"The sermon is the best weapon in th ·ry
thought, and our imaginations, captiv   \-
ing may be the quintessential theologic   ·
Ahmi Lee describes the two prevailing   ....ogical,
and proposes a third model, the dramat.   ...serves the best of the
other two (the emphasis on doctrine and life experience, respectively) while
avoiding their weaknesses. She rightly sees that the ministry of proclaiming God's Word is an invitation to disciples to enter into the historical
drama of Jesus Christ as actors who participate in this story made flesh.
Lee's proposal for a theodramatic homiletic provides pastors with the
tonic they need to communicate the gospel effectively to our increasingly
secularized, disenchanted age."

—**Kevin J. Vanhoozer**, Trinity Evangelical Divinity School

"Too many homiletics books frustrate readers with predictable and played
out hermeneutical scripts, such as the preacher-as-exalted-interpreter or
the preacher-as-humiliated-subject. Thankfully, Ahmi Lee breaks free from
these flat and stale patterns of description. *Preaching God's Grand Drama*
offers us a better script, a fresher performance than the typical proposals,
one that holds promise for preachers and for preaching both now and in
the future."

—**Jared E. Alcántara**, Truett Theological Seminary, Baylor University;
author of *The Practices of Christian Preaching*

"Ahmi Lee has provided us with a fresh way of looking at the task of
preaching. She calls us to acknowledge the 'theodramatic' nature of God's
work and our work in proclaiming the Word. For preachers who are weary
of having to choose either 'textual' or 'topical' preaching, *Preaching God's
Grand Drama* offers a profoundly rich vision that will inform and inspire
an alternative way of seeing that stretches the homiletical imagination to
more theologically fitting dimensions. This book is a wonderful example of
the kind of integrative thinking we urgently need to practice as preachers
and teachers of preaching. I hope it will be widely read."

—**Michael Pasquarello III**, Robert Smith Jr. Preaching Institute,
Beeson Divinity School, Samford University

"Pioneering new homiletical territory, Ahmi Lee's *Preaching God's Grand Drama* invites propositional preachers and conversational preachers to explore their respective sermonic philosophies and methodologies. Well-written and insightful, Lee's book presents an intriguing 'third way' explaining the art and craft of preaching that will meet and greet a wide spectrum of twenty-first-century listeners seated in the pews."

—**Matthew D. Kim**, Gordon-Conwell Theological Seminary; author of *Preaching with Cultural Intelligence*

"Ahmi Lee's vision of theodramatic preaching presents a lively and artful middle way between propositional and conversational preaching. By centering on an encounter with God in both the sermon and the world, Lee proposes a homiletic that encourages preachers to offer an essential balm for our wounded times."

—**Paul Scott Wilson**, Emmanuel College, University of Toronto

"In an effort to be serious about the Bible as the source of doctrinal truths, have we missed the forest for the trees? Have we atomized Scripture into so many disparate ideas that we have missed its central unifying drama? Ahmi Lee thinks so and wants to encourage pastors to preach the Bible as narrating a single dramatic story in which we are all characters as we dwell in Christ. The Bible narrates a cracking good story. And it is our story! Lee helps preachers perform this grand narrative in ways that will transform everyday lives in the light of God's ongoing dramatic actions in the world."

—**Scott Hoezee**, The Center for Excellence in Preaching, Calvin Theological Seminary

Preaching
God's
Grand Drama

Preaching God's Grand Drama

A Biblical-Theological Approach

AHMI LEE

FOREWORD BY MARK LABBERTON

Baker Academic
a division of Baker Publishing Group
Grand Rapids, Michigan

Published by Baker Academic
a division of Baker Publishing Group
PO Box 6287, Grand Rapids, MI 49516-6287
www.bakeracademic.com

Printed in the United States of America

Library of Congress Cataloging-in-Publication Control Number: 2019943031

ISBN 978-1-5409-6049-8
ISBN 978-1-5409-6238-6 (casebound)

In keeping with biblical principles of creation stewardship, Baker Publishing Group advocates the responsible use of our natural resources. As a member of the Green Press Initiative, our company uses recycled paper when possible. The text paper of this book is composed in part of post-consumer waste.

19 20 21 22 23 24 25   7 6 5 4 3 2 1

#1124682417

Contents

Foreword

Communication is a miracle, and not a frequent one. This is both my observation and my experience, and I bet it may also be yours. Understanding our endless and daily efforts in communication—offered and received—takes us through the family, the school, the neighborhood, the workplace, the public square, and the wider society. It is not that we entirely fail to communicate or I would not bother to write this sentence nor would you bother to read it. Our efforts in verbal communication, however, are always proximate, negotiated, tentative. Their lapses, gaps, or conflicts frequently find us out and can unfortunately lead us down many different trails of disappointment, disconnection, and distrust. Yet we must necessarily keep at it. After all, we are made for communion, which presupposes communication, one to another.

This underscores that the stakes are frequently high in our communication with one another: communion made, tested, refined, or broken. What greatly raises the bar and the hope for communication lies near to the staggering claims of John's Gospel, "In the beginning was the Word and the Word was with God and the Word was God. . . . The Word was made flesh and dwelt among us, full of grace and truth."

Christians dare to trust that the Word-made-flesh is the One whose very being is communion and whose will involves communication. It's only in light of this grounding theological reality that meaning, conveying, and understanding become possible. And if that is true for our daily interpersonal communication, how much more does it need to be so when anyone dares to try to communicate with and about God. The preacher knows this to the core.

What Dr. Ahmi Lee offers in this book is the chance to notice and to evaluate the conceptual frameworks that, consciously or not, shape the mind-set of the preacher and the presuppositions and experiences of the listeners. She lays out influences behind and around the predominant models of preaching, appreciating their value but underscoring their problems too. What Dr. Lee recognizes, and what I confirm from my own observations, is that many feel they are being expected to be epistemological trapeze artists!

On the one hand, many preachers grounded in an orthodox or evangelical expression of the church have confidence in the "recovery" process by which the Bible is interpreted: mining the text for what is "in it." The assumption is that the intended meaning can be found through wise, educated, careful retrieval. For listeners to such preachers, the expectation is about the stable or fixed character of meaning through the nature of the Bible in particular, and of language more broadly. The validation of the "authority" of the preacher is their evident success at recovery and translation to today's hearers. This is one epistemological trapeze.

On the other hand, a very different trapeze is the view that the Bible's meaning is assumed to be largely "in front" of the text, in the community and experience of readers or hearers whose context affects their reception of the text, and whose perspective, community, and social location "makes" today's meaning. With this trapeze, meaning moves from indeterminate to more determinate based on real-time interaction between preacher, readers, context, and text. The immediacy of experience and context is primary over (and sometimes against) the possible boundaries of the text or the tradition.

Both of the trapezes are in motion as the preacher prepares and preaches. The demands of history and the demands of relevance contrast and collide in various ways. The preacher, the congregation, or the context exercise pressure on the preacher and push easily toward opposite extremes of objectivity/history or subjectivity/relevance. Thus preachers can easily fail to benefit from a more nuanced combination that holds the two together, resisting reductionism and polarization. This dilemma is at play wherever preachers find themselves, whether urban or rural, whether mainline or independent, whether white or black, whether in the West or in the global South.

Where can the thoughtful preacher who cares about text and context, tradition and culture, objectivity and subjectivity turn for help in negotiating this epistemological tension? This explains why Dr. Lee turns in fresh directions to offer a significant alternative that recasts the assumptions of the whole preaching and communication exercise. Her incorporation of and reflection on Kevin Vanhoozer's model of God's theodramatic revelation is profound. Dr. Lee is not just performing an abstract homiletical exercise but is inviting all preachers into an engaging, personal, and pastoral alteration of heart and mind for the sake of receiving and participating in God's communication and community. This is why her work here is so important, even urgent.

At a time when the church's communication seems so muddled, compromised, or contradictory to those inside its bounds, let alone to those beyond it, Dr. Lee's work gives preachers a chance to try to reconceive and reform the paradigm and practices of preaching that shape this central practice in Christian formation. Since the biblical vision of the mission of God is fundamentally communicative and communal, her work here is provocative and constructive. I for one am very grateful for her work and believe many other preachers are and will be too.

Mark Labberton, president, Fuller Theological Seminary

Acknowledgments

Some very special people come to mind when I reflect on this project. I would like to take this opportunity to acknowledge them and express my gratitude for their support and encouragement, which made all the difference in writing this book. I am deeply grateful to Mark Labberton, who enthusiastically accepted my request to write the foreword and was one of my primary readers who spent long hours helping me sharpen my reflections on hermeneutics and preaching. The guidance and encouragement of Clayton Schmit have meant so much to me. I remember his willingness to connect by phone and sit with me for hours, combing through my writing with particular attention to the performance dimension of preaching. I am indebted to Kevin Vanhoozer, who has been a critical conversation partner from my early stages of research. I have benefited from not only his scholarship but also his generosity in sharing his time, reflections, and a number of papers, presentations, and unpublished manuscripts, which have tremendously enriched me professionally and personally. I owe special thanks to Joel Green, the former dean of the school of theology, who approved my sabbatical to work on the book and later connected me with Jim Kinney at Baker Academic. Meeting Jim has been a true gift. I am grateful for Jim's interest in publishing this book and for his wisdom in knowing when to encourage and push me throughout the project. My heartfelt thanks goes out to Melisa Blok for her remarkable editorial assistance, which made the entire process truly delightful. Great appreciation also goes to Jeremy Wells, Mason Slater,

Shelly MacNaughton, and the rest of the Baker team for their tireless and creative work in designing and promoting the book. Deserving a special mention is Susan Carlson Wood, editor of faculty publications for Fuller Seminary, who has been more than a skilled copyeditor but also a wise sounding board for me. To my dear parents, brother, and family: thank you for your love and support! Most of all, words cannot fully express my gratitude to my trustworthy husband and loyal best friend, Ryan. Thank you for always being up for an adventure with me.

Introduction

I have often found myself caught between things. I lived my childhood between the two cultures of my parents: the native Korean culture of my mother and the Japanese culture of my father, who, despite being ethnically Korean, was born and raised in Japan, and so in every other sense of the word is Japanese. I was further caught between the multiracial, multiethnic culture of my American foreign school in Japan and a complex fusion of Korean-Japanese culture at home. Upon my eventual arrival and new life in the United States, I found myself caught in a new challenge: navigating a new world as a third-culture kid from abroad who fully belonged with neither the American-born and -raised Asians nor the first-generation Asian immigrants. Even though I was brought up in an American educational system whose culture significantly shaped my childhood and teen years, as an immigrant to this country, I was neither a citizen who fully belonged here nor a tourist or student who had a sense of belonging in their home country.

This in-between cultural experience also captures my ecclesial experience, especially when it comes to preaching. For the greater part of my life, I was formed and nourished by pulpits that primarily aimed to exposit a biblical text as clearly as possible. Sermons had a chiefly catechetical function and could be summarized in a few logical and salient points that related to the text's central idea. My pastors spoke as great teachers and prophets who strove to hide themselves behind the Word in order to pass on only the decisive divine Word to the congregation, who would hear and obey it. This style of preaching more or less captures my theological training as a seminary student too. However, in my preaching journey I also encountered more recent homiletical literature (from the 1950s on) that advocates a different style of preaching: the sermon as a liturgical event that gathers the church around its central conversations. A pastor who prefers this way of preaching often likens his or her task to that of a storyteller, poet, or host—among a wide array of other creative metaphors—who evokes and invites listeners into a communal reality-shaping experience. Over time I realized something else: this is not just about my personal journey; many people relate to this experience. The two approaches to sermons that I describe appear everywhere and are thriving. As someone who preaches locally and in other parts of the world in diverse contexts, and as a teacher of preaching at a multidenominational evangelical seminary, I encounter many who are caught between these two prominent and prevalent "cultures" of preaching today. Preachers often side with one over the other; congregations seem to prefer one style instead of the other; and many preaching books fall into one of these two broad theological approaches. Whichever you are more familiar with or gravitate toward today, the point is that these two contrasting theories and practices of preaching dominate pulpits and classrooms near and far.

This book addresses the difficult in-between place that all of us in preaching today find ourselves. Whether you are a pastor, seminary student, layperson, or teacher of preaching, you likely find yourself caught between the two prevailing approaches: (1) the text-centered, so-called traditional preaching that is known for making bold, overarching claims since meaning is perceived as fixed in the biblical text, and (2) the more recent reader-centered, conversational mode of preaching that understands meaning as a collaborative construct of a local faith community and that is gaining interest and popularity in churches and in Christian academia. We are caught in a time and place where we discernibly feel the impact of philosophical and cultural postmodernism—in reaction to modernism—in our religious life. With the indubitable foundation of absolute truth deteriorating beneath our feet, many preachers desperately tighten their grip on the familiar notions of absolute certitude and authority in preaching. Others find new security in the communal experience of participating in the meaning-making of preaching. Many of us feel we are caught between the two: we must draw a hard line between modern objectivity and postmodern subjectivity and therefore preach as if we belonged exclusively to one side or the other. This kind of polarizing, all-or-nothing thinking is exacerbated by the "worship wars" of "conservative" and "liberal" debates and each group's favored preaching style.

Against this backdrop, the purpose of this book is twofold: first, to describe and critique the two homiletical approaches that correspond to the present shift in epistemology; and second, given the pernicious contrariety of these models, to propose a centered third approach that builds on both of their strengths. By identifying and assessing the underlying assumptions of these seemingly antithetical approaches to preaching, I hope to show the need for a harmonizing model of preaching that reconsiders the preacher's role in relation to the Bible, the congregation, and the world. Then, in order to address the gap created by the prevalent either/or approach to preaching in the current homiletical literature, I adopt theodramatic theology as a framework that can hold together divine authorial intention and freedom of readers, coherence and particularity of texts, and proposition and experience. The vision of preaching advanced in these pages proposes an integrative and formative theological activity that directs the whole church in light of God's own gracious past, present, and future performance in the world.

The following six chapters are structured to carefully consider each critical piece in this reflection. Chapter 1 provides an overview of the so-called traditional homiletic by surveying four metaphors that represent its theory and practice. The intent is not to be comprehensive but to name widely accepted customs in preaching and trace where they may come from, with the larger aim of assessing this model's strengths and weaknesses.

Chapter 2 broadly sketches the New Homiletic movement that is considered to be a shift away from the established habits of the traditional pulpit, and it focuses on the characteristics and assumptions of the conversational homiletic as advanced by Lucy Rose, John McClure, and O. Wesley Allen Jr. Although the ideas of these three scholars are distinct, at a basic level their approaches show striking similarity. Postmodern philosophy provides a larger backdrop for chapter 3, allowing us to uncover and focus on the inherent assumptions and values shared by all three conversational models. This chapter provides an extended critique because, while a number of books evaluate traditional preaching, no significant literature currently focuses on the phenomenon of conversational preaching that epitomizes the New Homiletic movement and the philosophical and cultural postmodernism in vogue. One of my major aims is to provide a much-needed deconstructive treatment of the conversational homiletic and, in doing so, highlight the limitation of its attempts to address the problems of the traditional model at the expense of what is not only central but also essential to preaching: trust in God's ability to communicate through Scripture.

Chapter 4 treats the disengagement of doctrine (the epic dimension) and life (the lyric) seen in the traditional and conversational styles of preaching. It then poses the question of whether biblical interpretation that preserves both the integrity of Scripture and the identity of readers is possible. In response to this query, the chapter proposes a "dramatic" view of theology as advocated by Hans Urs von Balthasar, N. T. Wright, Nicholas Lash, and most prominently, Kevin J. Vanhoozer. This view of theology is able to faithfully communicate the coherence and unity of the biblical discourse and its meaning and significance without sacrificing the complexities of perspectives, themes, and expressions present in it.

Chapter 5 imports dramatic theology into preaching and constructs a homiletic using the building blocks of its ideas. Considering the nature, purpose, and context of preaching, this chapter examines the contours of a theodramatic homiletic. It understands preaching as a performance of the gospel reality that reorients worldviews and values and ultimately moves the church to participate in the ongoing story of God. Although a number of important publications have appeared in the past several years that explore the nexus of theodrama and preaching, books that employ a theatrical framework for homiletical theology are, overall, sparse. This book makes a modest contribution to the emerging discussion by imagining what the ministry of the Word looks like through a dramatic theological lens that holds the epic of traditional preaching and the lyric of conversational preaching in dynamic tension. Finally, chapter 6 summarizes the characteristics of a theodramatic homiletic and suggests four perspectives that cultivate our attentiveness to the full range of God's story so we can participate wholly in his initiative and mission. Although the chapter includes ample questions to demonstrate the kind of work entailed in the four perspectives, the interest and scope of this book preclude discussions on methodology, sermon forms and language, and delivery. These topics remain fruitful areas for future research that will surely enrich the growing conversation on theodramatic preaching.

We are caught today between the various pressures and counterpoints already mentioned, but the greatest and the most significant tension in which we find ourselves is the *here* and *not-yet* reality of the kingdom. This book does not provide a definitive answer or a one-size-fits-all methodology for preaching in this complex in-between time. Instead, I ask you to join me in reflecting on God's story of what he has done, is doing, and will do—and in this light to consider how we might better live as strangers and exiles in this world. Whether you are very familiar with the homiletical landscape or are now just stepping out into unfamiliar territory, I hope that this book clearly sketches the terrain and gives you an idea of the dominant features that are worth our attention. Along the way, I ask you to reflect on where your preaching stands in relation to the two homiletical landmarks I describe and how you might benefit from this conversation. In this way, I am hopeful that we can wisely navigate together what it means for us to be "lived interpretations of Scripture"[1] until the day when Christ's kingdom is realized and his glory is fully revealed.

---

1. Kevin J. Vanhoozer, *The Drama of Doctrine: A Canonical Linguistic Approach to Christian Theology* (Louisville: Westminster John Knox, 2005), 349.

1

The Traditional Homiletic

Truth Mined, Truth Proclaimed

The rich heritage of Christian preaching reaches back to Old Testament prototypes of preachers like Noah, who was called a "preacher of righteousness" (2 Pet. 2:5), and Moses, who as a messenger participated in God's mission. It carries a weighty legacy of great Old Testament prophets like Deborah, Isaiah, Jeremiah, and Hosea, who delivered God's burning message of judgment and the promise of redemption to their contemporaries. Christian preaching reaches its glorious pinnacle in Jesus Christ, the incarnate God, whose very being "preaches" truth and grace to all with no partiality. Christian preaching follows in the footsteps of courageous disciples and apostles of faith—like Mary Magdalene, who first announced the joyful news of Jesus's resurrection, and Peter, who interpreted the miracle of tongues at Pentecost as a fulfillment of God's sovereignly ordained events that included Jesus's crucifixion and exaltation.

The heritage of preaching overflows with inspiring stories from the patristic era, when the ministry of the Word flourished through the works of preachers like Ambrose, Basil the Great, Augustine of Hippo, and John Chrysostom, who urged people to understand God rightly. Within this heritage is a treasury of missionary narratives of the Dominicans and Franciscans in the Middle Ages, who spoke against the vices of their time

and challenged people to pursue godliness and live holy lives for the common good of society. The story of the church's preaching also includes the
dramatic upheaval of the Reformation era, the blossoming season of the
pulpit during the Renaissance, and the tumultuous eras of modernity and
postmodernity characterized by radical shifts in thinking about reason,
progress, and ways of being. The richness and complexity of the heritage
of the pulpit extends far beyond what can be recounted here.

Notwithstanding the vast array of people and styles of preaching
throughout history, one particular oratorical approach rose in favor to
take prominence. Ironically referred to as the *traditional homiletic*, this
theory and practice of preaching does not so much represent the rich heritage of Christian preaching as demonstrate how parts of the legacy have
been emphasized and practiced over time. Bearing the nickname "three-
points-and-a-poem," traditional preaching is typically discursive and follows a well-recognized form in which one central idea is supported by a
few subpoints and punctuated by an emotionally appealing illustration.
Despite some variances of form, traditional sermons are generally propositional, deductive, and didactic. And whatever else may be said about
preaching's purpose, it is foundationally a ministry of teaching timeless,
divine truths from Scripture in a structured, linear manner. Concerning
this model of preaching, Lucy Rose notes, "One of the longest-standing,
dominant voices at the homiletical table is traditional or classical theory
that is grounded in homiletical rhetoric. . . . Throughout the nearly two
thousand years of Christian preaching, traditional theory has shifted its
boundaries and its emphases; yet much has remained the same."[1]

This chapter examines the so-called traditional homiletic and four metaphors that represent its most prominent traits. These metaphors (discussed
below) are the Herald, Banking Transfer, Golden Key, and Still-Life Picture. It needs to be noted that the metaphors and the label "traditional"
are limited at best because they do not account for the fecund diversity of
theological and homiletical perspectives, orientations, styles, and practices
throughout the church's history. Also, they are not exhaustive or precise
but serve only to highlight salient characteristics often associated with

---

1. Lucy Rose, *Sharing the Word: Preaching in the Roundtable Church* (Louisville: Westminster John Knox, 1997), 13.

the traditional model. In this sense, the metaphors sketch a "homiletical caricature" of sorts: some pronounced features and peculiarities of what has been considered "traditional" preaching are laid out for the ease of recognizing the abiding assumptions and practices of the pulpit. As is the purpose of caricature, these metaphors draw attention to the conspicuous markers of the Western pulpit and critique what is found lacking or perhaps needs more nuancing in light of preaching's rich legacy. Despite the clear limitation, the common term *traditional homiletic* and its variants in preaching literature (e.g., *traditional model, traditional preaching*) underscore the prevailing patterns of how preaching has been and continues to be understood, taught, and practiced.

This chapter lays the groundwork for the following chapter, which examines another approach to preaching—namely, conversational preaching, which is a reaction against the shortcomings of the traditional model. The first two chapters demonstrate the need for a third approach to preaching that draws from the strengths of both models while also addressing their weaknesses.

Four Metaphors: Key Assumptions of the Traditional Homiletic

Herald

Few metaphors more effectively capture the traditional preacher's understanding of the ministry of the Word than the *herald* metaphor. The imagery originates in the New Testament, with the Greek verb *kēryssō* appearing sixty-one times (e.g., Matt. 3:1; Acts 8:5; Rom. 10:8; 2 Tim. 4:2). The rich imagery of the herald metaphor involves three elements that pertain to the core convictions of the traditional homiletic.

First, the metaphor points to God as the external message-giver in a communication that involves the church. The source of the message is a self-communicating God who graciously discloses himself because he desires to be known. The traditional preacher's confidence rests on this God who has spoken and acted in history and whose nature is to be light, whose mission is to reveal and make himself accessible to us. Divine revelation is thus not only the sine qua non for preaching but also the sure footing that enables the preacher to stand and boldly claim to know something.

The traditional preacher would say, "We can know God because God has made himself known!" The sermon's effectiveness rests on the divine authority of the message.

Second, the herald metaphor paints the preacher as an emissary elected, equipped, and commissioned by God to make his will known. As glorious as it is to be a spokesperson for the King of kings, the herald is merely a messenger whose task is to faithfully pass on an entrusted message to a designated audience. The task demands that messengers not get in the way of the message and hence put aside their own ideas and biases, which could hinder others from hearing God's voice clearly. The herald must therefore be a pure channel that only transmits God's words to those who need to hear them. With the herald's great responsibility, however, also comes a great promise: God does not send out the messenger empty handed. Along with the Word to be shared, God confers authority, gifting, and anointing to his representative.

Third, the herald metaphor assumes that the congregation listens as willing recipients of the sermon. Since the preacher speaks on behalf of God, the congregation is expected to eagerly lean in to hear what the herald proclaims, to receive the word with humility, and to comply. Because God knows exactly what his people need to hear, the hearer's appropriate response to the sermon is openness and trust in both the message itself and the one who was sent by God to share it.

Banking Transfer

Another metaphor that represents the operating assumptions of the traditional homiletic is the *banking transfer*. This metaphor illustrates the traditional preacher's conception of preaching as a pedagogical activity that deposits knowledge in a unidirectional manner from the minister to the congregation.[2] Throughout history, numerous homileticians have offered their two cents about the purpose of the pulpit. Among countless words generated on this topic, one simple term has occupied the homiletical spotlight from the church's infancy: *teach*.

---

2. Drawing from Paulo Freire's discussion on pedagogical models, D. Stephenson Bond refers to the traditional homiletic as a "banking concept" model that is to be distinguished from a dialogical model of preaching that he advances. See D. Stephenson Bond, *Interactive Preaching* (St. Louis: Chalice, 1991), 58–60.

The link between preaching and teaching was forged early on. Even by the end of the first century, Christian preaching had cast itself as "a style of *homileō*-ing that exhorted listeners to live into the moral claims of the gospel while also offering theological teaching."[3] As the church continued to expand and encounter challenges of religious syncretism, the need to define Christian truths and doctrines and defend them against heresy and apostasy grew. So church leaders taught believers about the meaning of core Christian practices (e.g., worship, baptism, Eucharist) and about what is biblically sound. In such an environment, preaching was associated with salubrious instruction that guides people in ethical living informed by the gospel.

It was Augustine who formally equated preaching and pedagogy in what is widely considered the first homiletical manual, *De doctrina christiana* (*On Christian Doctrine* or *Teaching Christianity*). Augustine, drawing on his oratory background and applying the words of Cicero to preaching, states that the purpose of a sermon is to teach (*docere*), to delight (*delectare*), and to move (*movere*) listeners so they can do what is good and avoid what is bad in order to love God and neighbor. Of these three goals, Augustine deems the responsibility of educating listeners the most basic: "Instructing is a matter of necessity, delighting a matter of charm, and moving them a matter of conquest."[4] As a trained rhetorician, Augustine is well aware of the persuasive power of human words. His high theological view of divine beauty leads to his insistence that a sermon's form and style matter in pleasing hearers. But above all else, the preacher's duty is to be "the defender of the true faith and the opponent of error, both to teach what is right and to refute what is wrong, and in the performance of this task to conciliate the hostile, to rouse the careless, and to tell the ignorant both what is occurring at present and what is probable in the future."[5] Perhaps Augustine's strong emphasis on teaching is the reason traditional preaching is commonly associated with his name, even though many of his theological impulses and practices do not align neatly with the trademarks of the traditional approach.

3. Robert Reid, *The Four Voices of Preaching: Connecting Purpose and Identity behind the Pulpit* (Grand Rapids: Brazos, 2006), 38–39.
4. Augustine, *De doctrina christiana*, trans. R. P. H. Green (Oxford: Clarendon, 1995), 4.12.74.
5. Augustine, *De doctrina christiana* 4.4.6.

Following in Augustine's footsteps, Alan of Lille also describes preaching as the work of instruction and, in doing so, further solidifies the view of preaching as a didactical endeavor. In *The Art of Preaching*, Alan writes:

> Preaching is an open and public instruction in faith and behavior, whose purpose is the forming of men [*sic*]; it derives from the path of reason and from the fountainhead of the "authorities." . . . Preaching is that instruction which is offered to many, in public, and for edification. . . . By means of what is called "preaching"—instruction in matters of faith and behavior—two aspects of theology may be introduced: that which appeals to the reason and deals with the knowledge of spiritual matters, and the ethical, which offers teaching on the living of a good life. For preaching sometimes teaches about holy things, sometimes about conduct.[6]

To Alan, preaching is "more formative than transformative" in that it can "help to shape the theological and ethical understanding of people."[7]

To be precise, however, the connection between preaching and teaching existed prior to Augustine or Alan of Lille. After all, preaching in Jewish synagogue worship was primarily expository: a rabbi interpreted a passage of Torah and applied it to the lives of the listeners. In fact, this style of preaching is exemplified even in Origen (considered to be the first systematic theologian and homiletician), who gave a basic structure to Christian preaching that lasted until the Middle Ages.[8] Origen's sermons have a definite "form" in that they mostly follow one homiletical pattern, which is to systematically exegete the text like a running commentary. As a trained grammarian, Origen focused his preaching on explicating the Bible by offering various translations in the original languages and elucidating the passage well so that people could comprehend it. His emphasis on the literal sense is often overlooked because of his association with the Alexandrian method of spiritual-allegorical interpretation, but it was Origen who forged an enduring connection between preaching's

6. Alan of Lille, *The Art of Preaching*, trans. Gillian R. Evans (Kalamazoo, MI: Cistercian Publications, 1981), 16–17.

7. Joseph R. Jeter Jr., "Cultivating a Historical Vision," in *Teaching Preaching as a Christian Practice: A New Approach to Homiletical Pedagogy*, ed. Thomas G. Long and Leonora Tubbs Tisdale (Louisville: Westminster John Knox, 2008), 152.

8. O. C. Edwards Jr., *A History of Preaching* (Nashville: Abingdon, 2004), 31.

purpose and a grammarian's task of dissecting and expounding the text to discover meaning embedded deep within the sea of words. Guided by the signs of the Bible, the preacher's duty was to decipher the "code" of the text, ferret out the meaning within, and convey its significance to the hearers, who do not have the training to do so.

The relationship between teaching and preaching was formed early in church history and has endured until recent times. In 1870 John A. Broadus reaffirmed the affinity between teaching and preaching in his work *A Treatise on the Preparation and Delivery of Sermons*. In it, Broadus pays tribute to his predecessors, such as Augustine, as he promotes preaching as an educational endeavor. To Broadus, "the primary conception of preaching is to bring forth the teachings of some passage of Scripture,"[9] and, relatedly, the preacher's "very purpose is teaching and exhorting [people] out of the Word of God."[10] The teacher-preacher has a responsibility to "tell the people what to believe, and why they should believe it."[11] The preacher does this by conferring biblical truths to listeners' lives. For Broadus, "the application of the sermon is not merely an appendage to the discussion or a subordinate part of it, but is the main thing to be done."[12] As Broadus's book gained prominence as the standard textbook for preaching across seminaries in North America, preaching was further cast as the work of instruction that applies Scripture to listeners' lives—the prevailing concept of preaching until the rise of the "New Homiletic" in the 1950s.[13]

These examples offer a glimpse of one of preaching's long-standing foundational beliefs: to preach means to teach. As one who is called, elected, and trained, the preacher is responsible for instructing the congregation to live in accordance with God's statutes. Toward this end, the preacher searches the biblical text for meaning within the soil of ancient grammar, and once the preserved meaning is unearthed, the preacher must successfully transfer that wealth of knowledge to listeners without obscuring it.

9. John A. Broadus, *On the Preparation and Delivery of Sermons*, ed. Jesse Burton Weatherspoon (New York: Harper & Brothers, 1944), 87.

10. Broadus, *Preparation and Delivery*, 24.

11. Broadus, *Preparation and Delivery*, 146.

12. Broadus, *Preparation and Delivery*, 210.

13. Jesse Burton Weatherspoon later revised John A. Broadus's classic *On the Preparation and Delivery of Sermons*, but much of the former author's ideas were left unchanged.

Golden Key

The roots of preaching can be traced back to the ancient soil of Greco-Roman rhetoric. Because of a strong emphasis on persuasion and use of deductive reasoning, the traditional model often goes by the nickname "Aristotelian preaching." Given that primitive Christian preaching was crosscultural in nature, with a large number of non-Jewish audience members, early preachers had to adopt the prevailing communication style of the period to effectively reach their audience. Generally speaking, "Greco-Roman audiences would understandably expect public speeches to conform to the principles of appropriate civic discourse in the Empire, otherwise the message, regardless of how vital, would fall on deaf ears."[14] As such, classical rhetoric with its interest in clear and compelling argumentation became a pervasive influence on Christian preaching. O. C. Edwards Jr. suggests that Greco-Roman rhetoric may in fact be the single greatest influence on Christian preaching.[15] One of the lasting influences of classical rhetoric on Christian preaching is the view of the sermon as persuasive discourse, a *golden key* that opens the door to the listeners' understanding and their embrace of the message.

A few notable characteristics can be highlighted to account for the impact that Greco-Roman rhetoric has had on the shape of preaching as persuasive speech.[16] Take, for instance, the way many Western preach-

---

14. Lucy Hind Hogan and Robert Reid, *Connecting with the Congregation* (Nashville: Abingdon, 1999), 32.

15. O. C. Edwards, *History of Preaching*, 12.

16. This section does not cover an extensive history of Western Christendom. Instead, the present section draws attention to some examples of Greco-Roman rhetoric setting the trajectory of preaching. For detailed studies that trace the development of Christian preaching, see Hughes Oliphant Old, *The Reading and Preaching of the Scriptures in the Worship of the Christian Church*, 7 vols. (Grand Rapids: Eerdmans, 1998–2010); O. C. Edwards, *History of Preaching*; O. C. Edwards Jr., "History of Preaching," in *Concise Encyclopedia of Preaching*, ed. William H. Willimon and Richard Lischer (Louisville: Westminster John Knox, 1995); Richard Lischer, ed., *The Company of Preachers: Wisdom on Preaching from Augustine to the Present* (Grand Rapids: Eerdmans, 2002); DeWitte T. Holland, *The Preaching Tradition: A Brief History* (Nashville: Abingdon, 1980); Paul Scott Wilson, *A Concise History of Preaching* (Nashville: Abingdon, 1992); Michael Pasquarello, *Sacred Rhetoric: Preaching as a Theological and Pastoral Practice of the Church* (Grand Rapids: Eerdmans, 2005); and Edwin Charles Dargan's classic, *A History of Preaching*, 2 vols. (1905; repr., London: Forgotten Books, 2012). See also chap. 1 of Robert Reid, *The Four Voices of Preaching*. In the first chapter Reid provides a historical sketch of early Christian preaching, showing how the sermon as a structured argument has evolved over time.

ers are typically trained to prepare and deliver sermons. In many cases, seminaries draw from Aristotle's insight on the three modes of persuasion (i.e., *ethos*, *logos*, and *pathos*) when instructing preachers on the basics of speech. Coaching them to appeal to the credibility of the speaker, the reasonability of the arguments presented, and the sympathies of the listeners, preachers are taught to ground their sermons in these three pillars of communication.

It is also not uncommon for this lesson to be conjoined with the Ciceronian teaching on the five canons of an oratory task. The canons of *inventio* (invention), *dispositio* (arrangement), *elocutio* (style), *memoria* (memory), and *pronuntiatio* (delivery)[17] are often taught as rhetorical guidelines as preachers brainstorm what to say in the sermon, organize ideas to make a convincing case, contemplate speech styles, memorize content, and practice delivery.

Along with the teachings of Aristotle and Cicero, the anonymous work *Rhetorica ad herennium* serves as a common basis for instructing preachers. Preachers are taught that effective oration entails six parts of a speech—*exordium* (introduction), *narratio* (statement of facts), *divisio* (division), *confirmation* (proof), *confutatio* (refutation), and *conclusio* (conclusion).[18] When these parts are skillfully assembled, they build an argument that cannot be easily dismantled.

Such "rules of eloquence" have fashioned the church's understanding of the sermon as persuasive oration because many early Christian preachers were shaped by classical education. A survey of the first apostles shows that possessing an impressive educational background is not the distinguishing mark of the earliest preachers. However, as the church expanded throughout the world, education often came as a privilege associated with the position of a minister. As Christianity gained popularity and power under Constantine's rule, the church further received unprecedented favor and support from the state.[19] As one expression of that support, church

17. Cicero, *On Oratory and Orators*, trans. J. S. Watson (Carbondale: Southern Illinois University Press, 1986).

18. Cicero, *Rhetorica ad herennium*, trans. Harry Copland (Cambridge: Harvard University Press, 1954). Even though Cicero is noted as the author in the edition cited here, most rhetoricians today do not identify this work as written by him. The original author of the rhetorical teachings in this ancient text remains anonymous.

19. O. C. Edwards, *History of Preaching*, 27–28.

leaders received training in the highest classical education—in particular, in the art of rhetoric. With an incredible opportunity presented to them, early Christian preachers learned the rules of rhetoric and applied their training to the ministry of the Word.[20]

After all, it is not difficult to see a link between rhetoric and preaching. Rhetoric was civic art that trained and empowered everyday people to make their own appeals before the court of law. And if rhetoric is about "persuad[ing] an audience to respond to truth that had been discovered by reason,"[21] preaching in a fundamental sense shares a similar interest and burden. Like the forensic task of "proving" one's case in a court of law, Christian preachers had to stand before a burgeoning Greco-Roman world that was flourishing with rivaling religious systems and make a case for Jesus Christ. These preachers, who were raised and nurtured in the Hellenistic culture, "assumed that the gospel is to be preached" and that "rhetoric provides the appropriate instrument."[22]

This view of the sermon as persuasive discourse is one of the lasting influences of classical rhetoric on Christian preaching. Like a golden key that unlocks rigid, sealed doors, good preaching eases the inhibitions of listeners and convinces them not only to seriously consider the claims of the gospel but also to accept them as their own beliefs that direct how they live. Notwithstanding the work of the Holy Spirit, who is centrally responsible for this, the preacher as an orator plays a vital role in crafting and delivering a compelling message. The sermon should be strategically constructed with well-thought-out, tenable arguments that explicate biblical truths, and they should be communicated in ways that eliminate ambiguity and resonate with listeners intellectually, emotionally, and ethically. Broadus speaks to this idea when he equates preaching with sacred

20. This statement is not meant to deny that various perspectives also existed about what the relationship between preaching and rhetoric ought to be. Some, like Basil of Caesarea and Jerome, argued that Christian preaching, which deals with matters of truth, does not share common ground with the secular art of rhetoric, which aims to make plausible (probable) arguments. Others, like Augustine and Alan of Lille, challenged that view by contending that preaching, although a sacred task, has much to learn from the art of oration as it can sharpen the skills of preachers as public communicators. See Hogan and Reid, *Connecting with the Congregation*.

21. Craig Loscalzo paraphrases Cicero from *De inventione*. See Craig A. Loscalzo, "Rhetoric," in *Concise Encyclopedia of Preaching*, ed. William H. Willimon and Richard Lischer (Louisville: Westminster John Knox, 1995), 410.

22. Ronald E. Osborn, *Folly of God: The Rise of Christian Preaching* (St. Louis: Chalice, 1999), 410.

rhetoric that systematically explains, applies, argues, and illustrates bibli-cal truths[23] for the sake of winning souls. What is noteworthy about the classical view of persuasive rhetoric is the operating assumption that there is a universal reason (*logos*), a shared human experience (*pathos*), and a common sense of morality (*ethos*) that the orator can appeal to, and that entreating the listeners on these bases in a logical, ordered manner will convince them to accept the claims presented.

Still-Life Picture

In the traditional homiletic, the content of the sermon generally consists of principles, concepts, and insights that are carefully extracted from the Bible using tools of exegesis. In agreement with this view David Buttrick regards biblical truth like a *still-life picture*: the Scripture is treated "as if it were objectively 'there,' a static construct from which . . . [the preacher] may get something to preach on."[24] The efficacy of mining divine truths rides on whether preachers fully render themselves blank slates—ridding themselves of all possible biases (e.g., gender, cultural, experiential) that prevent them from objectively reading the text. The assumption is that if a preacher is successful, the exegetical excavation will yield a rich discov-ery of truths, and the preacher can then proceed to shape the sermon by summarizing the ideas gleaned into a propositional statement that best captures the thrust of the whole passage. For this reason, many sermons tend to take on a deductive form that begins with a single declarative statement that encapsulates the "big idea" of the passage, and then the central assertion is clarified and supported with additional points in the body of the sermon. Concerning this style of preaching, Fred Craddock observes that "the sermons of our time with few exceptions [have] kept the same form."[25]

Again, it is difficult to know exactly how or why certain qualities of early preaching left strong imprints in the lasting form of the traditional homiletic, but it was clearly not fortuitous. Various "moments" in preach-ing history compounded sediments of prominent beliefs and practices

23. See Broadus, *On the Preparation and Delivery of Sermons*.
24. David Buttrick, "Interpretation and Preaching," *Interpretation* 35 (January 1981): 49.
25. Fred Craddock, *As One without Authority*, 4th ed. (Nashville: Abingdon, 2001), 13.

over time. One of those moments might be linked to Augustine, who is commonly referred to by the nickname "the sign reader." Although so much can be said about Augustine's theology and preaching, this by-name is noteworthy in this discussion because it points to the bishop of Hippos's belief that preaching was a task of interpreting and explaining biblical signs. He emphasizes the importance of reading the signs correctly because they are indicators to deeper spiritual meaning and transcendent reality, which ultimately is a call to love God and others. Through literal and figurative interpretations, Augustine taught preachers to grasp the deeper theological significance of Scripture. "Augustine considered the Bible to be basically a book of signs that need to be interpreted. . . . [Augustine and others before the rise of the modern historical-critical method] really believed that the interpretations they came up with were what the passages meant, what God intended for them to learn from the words of the prophet or the apostle. . . . [Augustine] believed as a matter of faith that every word in the Bible had been put there by God to convey some meaning."[26]

A second notable moment that contributed to the shape of the traditional sermon came in the thirteenth and fourteenth centuries when a style of preaching known as *thematic* (also known as university, scholastic, or school) sermons sprang up. Popularized by the friars of that time, thematic preaching is considered the "first real homiletical form that was not just a shapeless verse-by-verse comment on a passage from the Bible."[27] Unlike homilies leading up to that point in time (cf. Origen), thematic sermons are characterized by a systematic division of points and subpoints that fall under the main theme of the text. Like a tree with multiple branches extending from the trunk, this style of preaching follows a distinct order of first establishing a clear theme that is derived from a biblical passage and subsequently expanding the theme into three or four parts that are "proven" in the process of delivering a sermon. Writing in this period, Robert of Basevorn endorses a "three point" style of sermons explaining that "a threefold cord is not easily broken."[28]

26. O. C. Edwards, *History of Preaching*, 108.
27. O. C. Edwards, "History of Preaching," 199.
28. Robert of Basevorn, "The Form of Preaching [1322]," in *Three Medieval Rhetorical Arts*, ed. James J. Murphy (Berkeley: University of California Press, 1971), 138.

Thematic preaching not only assumes that there is more or less one preferred meaning to the biblical text but also assumes that there is one preferred way to communicate it, which is a deductive approach. Since the relationship between language and the particular reality (truth) to which it corresponds is regarded as positive and evident, sermons are thought to be most effective when structured into a series of assertions that sustain an argument. Given its organization and structure, thematic sermons are generally abstract rather than concrete in content, favoring topics that relate to doctrine and Christian ethics over practical matters of life. As suggested by the well-known moniker "three-points-and-a-poem," the legacy of thematic sermons is easily observable even today. Many pulpits shaped by the traditional views on preaching have a penchant for methodically formatted sermons with supporting points that reinforce a theme rather than sermons that tend to be fluid or a posteriori in orientation (e.g., narrative or inductive).

A third moment in the development of the traditional preaching form can be connected to Martin Luther. Luther is widely known for his theological ideas, such as the five theological pillars of the Reformation; for his views on the law and grace and the written and spoken Word/word; and for his conviction about the priesthood of all believers. Yet Luther was as prolific a preacher and as influential a homiletician as he was a renowned theologian. If only one of his homiletical contributions had to be named, it would be his method of *die schriftauslegende Predigt*, or expository preaching.[29] Rather than expounding every word of a passage in a sequential manner or using a verse-by-verse approach as many before him had done, Luther believed that the purpose of preaching was to uncover and make plain the *Sinnmitte* (center of meaning), *Herzpunkt* (heart point), or *Kern* (kernel) of the passage.[30] The central thought of the text should be so evident that the rest of the sermon should follow from it, and the text's main idea is what the audience should remember in the end. His preparation also aligned with this style of preaching: "immers[ing] himself in the text and then preach[ing] extemporaneously, beginning

---

29. Fred W. Meuser, "Luther as Preacher of the Word of God," in *The Cambridge Companion to Martin Luther*, ed. Donald K. McKim (Cambridge: Cambridge University Press, 2003), 140.

30. O. C. Edwards, *History of Preaching*, 295.

with a statement of the *Herzpunkt* and going from there to extract that meaning from his text."³¹ With Luther's influence, preaching's aim became even more closely associated with the discovery and communication of one prominent meaning that is believed to exist between the words on the page. The import of Luther's homiletical contribution is the primacy of the propositional form championed by many traditional pulpits. Sermons are foremost fashioned by a single big idea that is derived from a passage.³² "Even though the traditional approach [allows] for a multitude of variation, the constant that [holds] them all together [is] the notion of the sermon as an idea, or proposition, and sermon form as the expression of the internal structure of that idea."³³

In the late nineteenth century, Philips Brooks added a fourth moment to the understanding of preaching when he defined the ministry of the Word as "the communication of truth by man to men [*sic*]." He asserted that sermons have "two essential elements, truth and personality," and "preaching is the bringing of truth through personality."³⁴ Rendering preaching as the communication of truth through personality, Brooks's words call to mind the long-standing influence of classical rhetoric on preaching, in particular, the Aristotelian teaching on *logos*, *pathos*, and *ethos* as the necessary modes of effective oration. More noteworthy, however, is Brooks's perception of truth as "a fixed and stable element."³⁵ As if the Bible contains deposits of timeless divine truths, Brooks's understanding of preaching suggests that the Bible contains a permanent and final meaning for preachers to simply tap into and draw out. Since biblical truths are

31. O. C. Edwards, "History of Preaching," 205.
32. Another giant of the Reformation, John Calvin, shared a similar view. He saw the written Word as perfect and as having no unnecessary word in it. He believed that the responsibility of the preacher was thus to divulge the original meaning of the biblical authors through exegesis and diligent study of the original languages. In this process, he trusted that the Spirit, who superintended the writing of the Scriptures, would guide the preacher to sound interpretation that ties in with the unity of the entire Bible. See H. Jackson Forstman, *Word and Spirit: Calvin's Doctrine of Biblical Authority* (Stanford, CA: Stanford University Press, 1962), and T. H. L. Parker, *Calvin's Preaching* (Edinburgh: T&T Clark, 1992).
33. Thomas G. Long, "Form," in *Concise Encyclopedia of Preaching*, ed. William H. Willimon and Richard Lischer (Louisville: Westminster John Knox, 1995), 147.
34. Philips Brooks, *Lectures on Preaching* (New York: Dutton, 1877), 5.
35. Thomas G. Long, "New Focus for Teaching Preaching," in *Teaching Preaching as a Christian Practice: A New Approach to Homiletical Pedagogy*, ed. Thomas G. Long and Leonora Tubbs Tisdale (Louisville: Westminster John Knox, 2008), 7.

seen as constant, the only variable in preaching is the personality of the minister. In other words, the personality and the communication ability of the preacher function as vehicles that relay the unchanging truth of God to people. Thus, "every preacher, whether in the pulpit next door or in a missionary congregation on the other side of the globe, preached the very same truth. The truth [is] a constant poured into the variable mold of human personality."[36]

Albeit a sampling, these examples help us understand the basic assumptions and values of the longest-standing practices of the pulpit. Those who subscribe to these views and practices tend to see Scripture as a minefield of predeposited truths. The preacher's task is to unearth what lies in the text by means of textual analysis and, upon identifying what is central to the passage—call it a "nugget," "main idea," or "thrust"—communicate its significance and applications in an ordered manner to listeners.

An Assessment of the Traditional Homiletic

Chapter 2 will survey the works of three prominent scholars who challenge the assumptions of the traditional preaching model. Examination of their works will give further attention to assessing the traditional homiletic. For now, consider a brief assessment focusing on three main areas of its strengths and weaknesses. These are presented as familiar Christian expressions: "Thus saith the Lord"; "the Bible tells me so"; and "And all God's people said, 'Amen.'"

Thus Saith the Lord

The expression "Thus saith the Lord" captures both the strength and the weakness of the traditional homiletic. The strength of traditional preaching is its foundational theological conviction that God has spoken and acted in history and that God delights to make himself known. God is ultimately incomprehensible but knowable. In fact, knowledge of God is essential for faith (Rom. 10:17). The focus on God's prior words and actions, which precede the minister's words and actions, is paramount, not

36. Long, "New Focus for Teaching Preaching," 7.

least because preaching's content and significance are grounded in God, who sought sinners out. Without God's grace-filled words and actions in history (because he did something we did not merit), there is no real message to be shared—at least not one that matters or can save eternally perishing sinners. We have a message to share with the world because God has really *done* something on our behalf. God's kind initiation, resolute love, and untiring faithfulness toward his contumacious children supply the preacher not merely with the necessary confidence to stand up and speak but also, more important, with real good news that is worth heralding to the world. In addition, the recognition of the authority and goodness of God as history's first communicator—as a totally free, independent communicative agent who is *other* than anyone or anything in this world—is what allows the church to be open and receptive to whatever message comes to us. Whether the message is one of hope or sorrow, blessing or wrath, comfort or admonition, the church can have quiet confidence and humility to listen, love, and fear what God says to us when we remember who he is and what he has first done for us.

Despite this strength, one danger of the traditional view of preaching is the potential to equate what flows from the pulpit with the very words of God—*viva vox Dei* directly addressing the people of God. The individual minister is typically the premier—if not the only—interpreter and proclaimer of what the Scriptures mean for the whole church. It is considered the minister's responsibility to protect the integrity of the gospel and the Scriptures' sacrosanctity by instructing the laity on the proper interpretations of texts. To do so, ministers scour the text for meaning using specialized tools from their training and, upon discovery, make universal application that connects with listeners' lives. In this sense, ministers in the traditional model "speak as persons who have been certified to explain meaning authoritatively"[37] for the whole church. The congregation is entirely dependent on the preacher to hear and discern on their behalf what God is saying to them.

The tremendous power that accompanies the pulpit and the minister's unique training and position above others also come with a great risk. Preaching has the potential to degenerate into a human campaign that

---

37. Reid, *Four Voices of Preaching*, 54.

promulgates the minister's personal assumptions, beliefs, and biases and further subjugates the congregation with "exegetical weapons." Accountability for the preacher who is above the rest of the faith community as a spiritual mediator between God and God's people is limited at best. Standing between God and God's people, the preacher is seen as a problem solver who supplies answers to life's conundrums in the form of sermons. Such a view is unrealistic and hazardous insofar as it promotes a self-centered and need-based theology of worship and preaching. Further, such a view is fundamentally antithetical to what ministers are called to be. "If to be in Christ and to give ourselves more and more to [God's] service is to realize a fuller humanity and to participate more fully and freely in the life which he redeems, then to become a minister is not to be placed in a special class but rather to be with humankind and in the world more fully and unreservedly, and to move as openly and easily in the world as grace allows."[38]

The Bible Tells Me So

"Jesus loves me! This I know, for the Bible tells me so!" These words from a beloved hymn capture another strength of the traditional view of preaching: a high view of Scripture. Like the old hymn says, the Bible to the traditional preacher is the unshakable ground on which believers can stake their claim to know something about God (e.g., "Jesus loves me"). God not only has spoken and acted in history but also has *revealed* himself to us in the person of Jesus Christ and through the continuing ministry of the Holy Spirit, who testifies about God foremost through the Scriptures. Therefore to the traditional preacher, Scripture is the ultimate source of authority—an inspired and preserved instrument of divine communication that is as trustworthy as it is essential for the church to have a right relationship with God. In a shifting and turbulent world that insists on the impotence of texts and the irrelevance of the author, the traditional preacher's safeguard is not a magnetic personality or many talents and abilities but trust and reliance on God's ability to graciously communicate and self-disclose, even through frail human words.

38. Charles L. Rice, "The Preacher's Story," in *Preaching the Story*, ed. Edmund A. Steimle et al. (Eugene, OR: Wipf & Stock, 1980), 25.

The traditional preacher's high regard for Scripture's authority relates to another strength: an emphasis on vigorous historical-critical study of the Bible that lends to sound and responsible interpretation. The task of the traditional preacher is to hear what the Bible intends to say (or to hear God, who appropriates himself to the language of Scripture) rather than to read meaning into it. To this end the preacher strives to exegete, or "draw out," the plain meaning of the text by investigating its historical context, literary makeup, and theological import in line with the church's "rule of faith." An analytic, systematic study of the text keeps the minister accountable to interpretive guidelines that protect Scripture's freedom and ability to address the church so its message can be heard within the proper context.

Yet a shortcoming of the traditional homiletic lies in reducing the awe-inspiring mystery of divine revelation to mere propositions ("the Bible tells me so"). The point here is not to debase propositions. Indeed the Bible does make determinate truth claims about God, the world, and human beings, which in their objective truthfulness have a real consequence for every person, who must choose to believe and accept or to doubt and deny. If the Bible contained no propositional content, there would be nothing the church is called to believe, to adhere to, or to preserve. Even so, the gospel cannot be reduced just to propositions, because it is so much more. The gospel is not simply an idea or a concept but a *reality* of God's kingdom that is here, made evident and available to us through Jesus Christ. To convey the grand reality of this God and his reign, which resists being "reduced to what human reason [can] manage,"[39] Scripture provides a kaleidoscopic witness, using a wide range of literary forms and styles that speak to us in different ways. However, the problem is that the preoccupation with propositions can treat stories, images, and metaphoric and poetic language

39. I agree with Alister McGrath's interpretation of C. S. Lewis's work The Chronicles of Narnia. McGrath notes that Lewis's depiction of Aslan (symbolizing Christ) goes against the trends of his day that "[impoverish] the majesty and mystery of Christ" either through preaching that makes Jesus too homely or through theology that tries to reduce Jesus into manageable doctrinal formulas (93). Aslan is kind but is not a tame lion. Lewis's portrayal of Aslan challenges the Enlightenment notion that "reality [can] be reduced to something that reason can master" (95) and invites readers instead to "see that Aslan should be appreciated as a totality [through the story], not simply reduced to a mere theory" (94). See Alister McGrath, *If I Had Lunch with C. S. Lewis: Exploring the Ideas of C. S. Lewis on the Meaning of Life* (Carol Stream, IL: Tyndale, 2014), 92–95.

as if the propositions that can be extracted from them convey what they mean—or convey all that they mean. Rather than appreciating the Bible as a totality, we can read it to extract the "kernel" of meaning (the cognitive content of principles, doctrines, and rules) and discard the "shell" of the biblical text. This approach results in stripping the multidimensionality of Scripture and diminishes it to "on-the-page inert language from which something may be removed and talked about."[40] When we do this, God's revelation is treated as "a source book for objective propositions, its stories viewed simply as illustrations of an ideational world of religious truths,"[41] and exegesis as "an illusion rather than the reality of listening to the text."[42] Ignoring the poetic and evocative language of Scripture also leads to the view of preaching as a rationalistic and cognitive endeavor and underplays the vital role of imagination in sermons.

In a similar vein, it is dangerous to equate the role of sermons to simply mining old truths from the Bible because it can breed two dysfunctions. First, while this view encourages diligent research into what the text once meant to the original audience, it neglects attentiveness to God, who continues to speak to the church through Scripture and by the activities of the Holy Spirit. In this view, God's work is treated as belonging exclusively to the past or, at a minimum, as if God's ministry in the Bible and in our world today is disparate and discontinuous. When preachers do not help congregations wrestle with how Scripture is continually and progressively being fulfilled in our day toward the grand finale of history, we fail to point people to God's enduring faithfulness and the power of his Word, which is meant to be savored here and now. Grasping the ancient context and the original meaning of the text is indispensable to hearing the Scriptures as intended, but a joyful expectation for how God may speak to us again using those same words is also essential to reading Scripture faithfully as God's dynamic, living Word.

The second and related dysfunction is that application is treated as an accessory to a sermon rather than an important hermeneutical lens that

40. David Buttrick, "Preaching the Christian Faith," *Liturgy* 2, no. 3 (1982): 54.
41. Richard L. Eslinger, *A New Hearing: Living Options in Homiletic Method* (Nashville: Abingdon, 1987), 134.
42. Fred Craddock, *Preaching* (Nashville: Abingdon, 1985), 100, quoted by Eslinger, *New Hearing*, 134.

guides the church's reading of Scripture. We read the Bible not to rehearse the past and affirm previous interpretations but to seek guidance on how we may live in God's present and into the future he intends. At times, this requires reformulating our prior understandings and interpretations in light of a more expansive and cumulative view of what God is doing through Christ in his Spirit. Not that the contemporary context should dictate the hermeneutical process but that biblical hermeneutics should bring the historical understanding and the present contextual understanding into a critical dialogue. Sermons without this kind of lively engagement tend to be driven by information that relates to *what* and *how*, and they are disconnected from listeners because the fundamental question of *why* something matters at all is not addressed.[43] Such sermons might temporarily fix people's behaviors but often fall short of generating a lasting transformation that is fueled by a changed heart and mind.

And All God's People Said, "Amen"

The driving agenda of the traditional homiletic is to teach God's precepts by expositing Scripture and by underscoring and affirming assertions "warranted" by the biblical text. The strength of traditional preaching is that it takes seriously the critical function of sermons to instruct the church. If indeed "faith comes from hearing, and hearing through the word of Christ" (Rom. 10:17), it seems that whatever else may characterize preaching as the ministry of the Word, the aspect of catechism is indispensable. The minister's basic assignment is to edify the church through biblical instruction.

Another notable strength of the traditional homiletic lies in its ability to "solicit from listeners the final affirmation, 'Yes! This is what we believe.'"[44] In other words, "And all God's people said, 'Amen.'" Speaking from "a hard core of convictions related to the historically theological

---

43. Interestingly, ethnographer and organizational expert Simon Sinek agrees that most effective leaders inspire and inject passion in others by helping them understand *why* something matters. In his own words, "People don't buy what you do; they buy why you do it, and what you do simply serves as the proof of what you believe." Simon Sinek, "How Great Leaders Inspire Action," TEDx video, September 2009, TEDx Puget Sound, 14:48, https://www.ted.com/talks/simon_sinek_how_great_leaders_inspire_action/transcript.

44. Reid, *Four Voices of Preaching*, 63.

and doctrinal convictions of the community,"[45] the traditional model of preaching generates social cohesion and solidarity that enable the church to cherish and cling to its shared beliefs.

Notwithstanding, this very strength of the traditional pulpit can turn into a dangerous pitfall when preaching serves only to sustain an ecclesial culture. Rather than disrupting the status quo and exposing pride and other self-serving forms of evil, preaching can become the means to maintain the community's imperturbable beliefs and habits. Furthermore, since the minister has the final authority on what the Bible means, the pulpit can become the platform to silence those whose experiences and thoughts differ from those of the minister or the dominant culture. Robert Reid observes, "Even if a sermon in [the traditional] voice concludes with an invitation to respond or to take action, the purpose of speaking in this voice is to invite the listener to accept the cultural consciousness implicit in this kind of talk."[46]

The problem is that if preaching's only aim is to reiterate what the church already believes to be true, there is little room for the congregation to share fresh insights, push back on the preacher's understanding of the text, or simply marvel at the mysteries of faith. The congregation is reduced to passive listeners who—although they affirm the preacher's message and may be active in that affirmation—have nothing to share or contribute to the ongoing understanding of God's Word.

Another danger of the traditional homiletic is the tendency to flatten the robust calling of preaching to a monolithic activity of teaching or a conveyance of ideational content. Preaching is certainly more but nothing less than "truth-sharing," a communication of information pertaining to an actual state of a matter. Yet preaching does not end with intellectual consent to truth; the goal is eliciting "truthful living" (genuine worship) from all who confess the lordship of Jesus Christ. As Augustine said, preaching is multidimensional work that teaches (speaks to the mind), delights (speaks to the heart), and, ultimately, moves people to live rightly in the world as Jesus's disciples (speaks to the action). Instruction is thus essential to preaching, but there is no sermon if the preacher fails to stir

45. Reid, *Four Voices of Preaching*, 63.
46. Reid, *Four Voices of Preaching*, 54.

desires, feelings, and imagination for an alternate way of living that directs people to live out their faith in accordance with Scripture.

The traditional homiletic is also susceptible to another weakness: the delimitation of the sermon form. While the traditional model emphasizes "good exegesis," which includes paying attention to the nature and stylistic elements of texts, once the "nugget" of the passage is identified, these considerations are pushed to the side and do not play a role in shaping the sermon. Whether the text is a poem or a letter, a chronicle or a parable— all texts are more or less treated the same when it comes to sermon design. Sermons are generally forced into the mold of "big idea" preaching that advances a single idea or proposition buttressed by a few subpoints. The problem is that this predetermined, one-size-fits-all approach to the sermon severely limits the communication of Scripture from the pulpit. When preachers package all messages and texts in a single sermon style, more is at stake than a chance to reach diverse listeners who process what they hear differently.[47] Preachers can miss the opportunity to be witnesses to the rich beauty of God's incarnational Word, which is communicated in various literary genres, forms, and styles. In order for preaching to be communication that goes beyond telling people *what* to say and do and trains the church *how* to think by reading the Bible well, the pulpit must seize every opportunity to model love and respect for God's Word even in the way sermons are shaped and delivered. We must honor not only what God says in the Bible but also how God in his beauty and wisdom has communicated to us in diverse voices and styles.

Conclusion

Preaching's rich heritage includes the beliefs and practices preserved and passed down that this chapter has discussed. Despite various social adversities, persecution, threats of heresies, and constant pressure from the world to conform, the preachers of old remained steadfast in their calling, and their legacy offers us an invaluable treasure that enriches our imagination for how we too might preach the gospel boldly in our own time. The

47. See Joseph R. Jeter Jr. and Ronald Allen, *One Gospel, Many Ears: Preaching for Different Listeners in the Congregation* (St. Louis: Chalice, 2002).

aspects of their legacy that have been most emphasized and remembered through history have become long-standing assumptions and practices of the Western pulpit. Many appear under the banner of the traditional homiletic, although they are not exclusive qualities of that particular style of preaching.

This chapter has surveyed some of the strengths and weaknesses associated with the traditional model of preaching. The greatest strength is the unfaltering trust in God's communicative ability to reveal himself and minister to his people through the reliable witness of Scripture. The preacher's confidence rests in the belief that God, who took the first step by making himself known to those who otherwise cannot know him, is the one who guides the preacher's study of Scripture and supplies the words to share with the church. In this respect, the preacher sometimes speaks as a herald sent out by God and other times speaks as a holy teacher whose task is to instruct and build up the church.

Despite these strengths, the traditional view of preaching also contains weaknesses and dangers. These include the preacher's misuse of authority, indifference to the culture of listeners, misconstruction of the idea that preaching is only concerned with God's past activities, perpetuation of an insular ecclesial culture, diminishment of Scripture's multidimensionality, minimizing the robust calling that is preaching, and delimitation of the sermon form. This critique does not imply a simple causal relationship between the traditional preaching model and certain problems in the pulpit. Rather, the critique hopefully highlights aspects of preaching that deserve (greater) attention because we may have overlooked or forgotten other theological convictions and practices that are also part of our rich faith heritage.

In hopes of addressing these blind spots and shortcomings, some around the homiletical table have named different assumptions and values that give shape to a different understanding of preaching—namely, they advocate a democratic approach to the sermon in which the preacher and the congregation together explore and experience the Word-event, rather than an authoritative one-way communication that flows from the pulpit to the pew. To their voices we turn in the following chapter.

2

The Conversational Homiletic

Communal Meaning-Making

A lthough a cursory glance at pulpit practice near and far reveals the widespread use of the three-points-and-a-poem type of deductive, pedagogical sermon, the culture and field of homiletics have been changing in recent decades. The shifts in the culture and preaching have called into question the relevance and efficacy of a univocal and unilateral sermon paradigm. This chapter turns to three key voices that challenge the traditional model's dominance on the homiletic stage: Lucy Rose, John McClure, and O. Wesley Allen Jr. These recent homileticians see preaching as a fluid, meaning-making conversation about Scripture to which the entire ecclesial body contributes: the conversational model. This chapter begins by sketching the larger context of their works and then surveys the specific proposals of these three thinkers. The next chapter is dedicated to an extended critique of the conversational model and its inherent assumptions and values, which are shaped by philosophical and cultural postmodernism.

Time Ripe for Change

The traditional homiletic reigned over the homiletical landscape for the greater part of Christian history. As noted in the previous chapter, *traditional homiletic* refers to discernible traits and patterns in preaching that have largely been accepted as customary. The traditional homiletic gained a wider prevalence and renewed momentum in 1870, when John A. Broadus published his monumental work *A Treatise on the Preparation and Delivery of Sermons*.[1] In this preaching manual, Broadus follows in the footsteps of Augustine and his first homiletical textbook by continuing to coalesce classical rhetorical principles and the practice of preaching. Broadus defines homiletics simply as "adaptation of rhetoric to the particular ends and demands of Christian preaching."[2] From his depiction of preaching to the promotion of rhetorical elements that are considered necessary in a sermon, Broadus's influential writing affirmed and further solidified the shape of traditional preaching. His work received wide acceptance across North America and even became a standard pedagogical tool for preaching. This traditional model dominated the homiletic terrain mostly unchallenged until the 1950s.

Then, in the 1960s and 1970s, preaching hit a crisis. Even through the detrimental effects of World War I and the depression that followed, numerous Christians persevered unwaveringly in their faith.[3] The sense of spiritual resolution more or less continued through the hardships of World War II.[4] Yet since then, as pluralism and postmodernism gained a stronger pulse and momentum in the culture, preaching that was grounded in foundationalism seemed outdated and ill suited to reach the public. Preaching was a glorious but declining art form that was losing its appeal amid a developing culture. John Stott believes that the low esteem for preaching at the time may have had something to do with the antiauthority mood of the culture (resulting from postmodern philosophy), the beginning of the cybernetics revolution that competed for people's attention (because oral communication was regarded as ineffective), and the church's overall loss of confidence in

1. John A. Broadus, *On the Preparation and Delivery of Sermons*, ed. Jesse Burton Weatherspoon (New York: Harper & Brothers, 1944). Broadus's original work was published in 1870 under the title *A Treatise on the Preparation and Delivery of Sermons*. Since then, it has gone through multiple revisions (over twenty by 1900) and is still in print given its demand. The influence of this work has been far reaching, even being translated into Chinese for its use in missions schools. It is a classic and a seminal work in the field of homiletics.
2. Broadus, *Preparation and Delivery*, 10.
3. John Stott, *Between Two Worlds: The Challenge of Preaching Today* (Grand Rapids: Eerdmans, 1982), 40.
4. Stott, *Between Two Worlds*, 42.

the gospel as skepticism filled the air.[5] Be that as it may, Thomas Long's metaphoric depiction of preachers in crisis in any generation portrays what many in this period have felt: "What happens is that the trusted structures and strategies of the pulpit suddenly seem to lose their potency, and worried preachers, their confidence shaken, begin to scramble for the next, new thing. After decades of gliding blithely across the homiletical dance floor to the same familiar rhythms, it dawns on preachers that the music has changed, culturally and theologically, and they are out of step. The usual techniques, customary homiletical tactics, and prevailing assumptions about the task of preaching all seem questionable or even dubious."[6]

As North American pulpits and pews languished and grew restless in light of rapid philosophical and cultural changes, the time was ripe for some kind of remaking in the field of preaching. In this momentous time, a radical paradigm shift took place in preaching that is now referred to as the New Homiletic.[7] Paul Scott Wilson remarks, "Not since the Middle Ages or the Reformation have such mighty winds swept the homiletical highlands"[8] as in this season of change.

The New Homiletic: A Celebration of Diverse Preaching Models

The beginning of the New Homiletic is often debated. The exact date and cause of its inauguration are difficult to pin down, since its ascent is interconnected with myriad social, historical, literary, and philosophical factors. Paul Scott Wilson contends that it was H. Grady Davis's writing *The Design for Preaching* that became the catalyst for the movement.[9] Davis challenges the normative view of the sermon as a sequential argument constructed by the preacher to support a central claim. In contrast, he likens the sermon to a tree[10]—an organic entity with a life of its own able to grow

---

5. Stott, *Between Two Worlds*, 50–89.

6. Thomas G. Long, *Preaching from Memory to Hope* (Louisville: Westminster John Knox, 2009), xiii.

7. David James Randolph receives the recognition for first coining the term *New Homiletic*, in *The Renewal of Preaching* (Philadelphia: Fortress, 1969).

8. Paul Scott Wilson, *The Practice of Preaching* (Nashville: Abingdon, 1995), 12.

9. H. Grady Davis, *The Design for Preaching* (Philadelphia: Fortress, 1958).

10. To be accurate, H. Grady Davis was not the first person to use the metaphor of a tree. It was Jacobus de Fusignano, a Dominican priest, who first likened the sermon to a tree back in 1310. Although both men used the same metaphor, a crucial difference exists between Fusignano's and

and expand over time. As the seed provides the building blocks for what is to come from it, so, as Davis asserts, sermons organically "grow out" from the intrinsic life and form of the biblical text. Davis's work was subversive in that he shifted the prevailing interest in homiletics from sermon content to sermon form,[11] and he showed that the content is inseparable from the form and thus the sermon need not be artificially forced into one template.

Following Davis's pioneering work,[12] in 1969 Fred Craddock published *As One without Authority*, which contributed to further expanding the familiar horizons of homiletics. Here Craddock contends that authority is not centralized in the preacher because the minister is just another member of the faith community who experiences God's Word alongside others.[13] In line with this belief, he advises induction as an effective method for preaching (i.e., moving from the particulars of human experience to conclusions about a general truth) because he believes that listeners are "capable of attending to the text, handling some scholarship, dealing with open-ended stories, and drawing [their] own conclusions."[14] Preachers should not try to spoon-feed and coerce listeners into believing something and should instead invite them to feast on the text as free agents who are capable of self-discoveries that incite genuine change.

About a decade later, Eugene Lowry published his work *The Homiletical Plot*, in which he argues that the key to sermonic experience is anticipation. To him, the sermon is not "a doctrinal lecture" but "an event-in-time, a narrative art form more akin to a play or novel in shape than to a book."[15]

Davis's depictions of what a sermon should look like. Fusignano's understanding of the sermon was largely propositional and deductive: from one central theme extends three points that support the main idea. In contrast, when Davis relates the sermon to a tree, he underscores the organic nature of a sermon in which the content shapes the form, not the other way around.

11. Charles Campbell, *Preaching Jesus: The New Directions for Homiletics in Hans Frei's Postliberal Theology* (Eugene, OR: Wipf & Stock, 1997), 117.

12. Thomas Long refers to H. Grady Davis's *Design for Preaching* as a "bridge spanning the gap between the traditional approach to form and those developments yet to come. . . . Davis was the bridge; homiletical theory has crossed over to the other side, and the primary category is no longer the structure of the idea, but the dynamics of the ear." See Thomas Long, "Form," in *Concise Encyclopedia of Preaching*, ed. William H. Willimon and Richard Lischer (Louisville: Westminster John Knox, 1995), 147–48.

13. Fred Craddock, *As One without Authority*, 4th ed. (St. Louis: Chalice, 2001).

14. Barbara Brown Taylor, foreword to Fred Craddock, *The Collected Sermons of Fred Craddock* (Louisville: Westminster John Knox, 2010), xi.

15. Eugene L. Lowry, *The Homiletical Plot: The Sermon as Narrative Art Form* (Atlanta: John Knox, 1980), xx.

So preachers should speak as skilled "narrative artists" who help listeners experience the biblical text. The key, according to Lowry, is building listeners' anticipation through the plotted movement of conflict, thickening of plot, foreshadowing of resolution, climactic experience of resolution, and conclusion that reflects back on the significance of what has happened in the story. Good preaching is similar to hearing a good story in that listeners remain engaged throughout and are powerfully impacted by a surprising reversal of events at the end, which makes for a memorable experience.

David Buttrick also contributed to the exciting changes in the field of preaching by penning *Homiletic*. Buttrick urges preachers to be more listener focused in their sermon designs by paying attention to how people listen, perceive, and process ideas. He calls how the human consciousness conjoins ideas *phenomenology*. Like photographic snapshots that are visualized and processed as a whole in a motion picture, he explains that people's perception of reality is constructed through a series of logical "moves" in a sermon. The aim in preaching is to use language to "rename the world 'God's world'" and to "change identity by incorporating all our stories into 'God's story.'"[16]

Besides Davis, Craddock, Lowry, and Buttrick, many others also pushed the boundaries of how preaching was commonly understood. Henry Mitchell, for example, believes that the sermon is a celebration-event in which the preacher and the congregation together are "[caught] up in an unforgettable experience"[17] of the dynamic Word. To Edmund Steimle, Morris Niedenthal, and Charles Rice, the sermon is a "shared story" in which the biblical story, the preacher's personal story, and the individual stories of listeners all come together.[18] Leonora Tubbs Tisdale supplied a new metaphor for preaching by comparing it to the work of an ethnographer in a foreign culture.[19] In addition to biblical exegesis, she urges preachers not to neglect exegesis of the congregational subculture so that sermons can be local expressions of theology for a particular congregation. Around the same time, Charles Bartow presented a theology of

16. David Buttrick, *Homiletic: Moves and Structures* (Philadelphia: Fortress, 1987), 11.
17. Henry H. Mitchell, *Celebration and Experience in Preaching* (Nashville: Abingdon, 1990), 66–67.
18. Edmund A. Steimle, Morris J. Niedenthal, and Charles L. Rice, *Preaching the Story* (Eugene, OR: Wipf & Stock, 2003).
19. Leonora Tubbs Tisdale, *Preaching as Local Theology and Folk Art* (Minneapolis: Fortress, 1997).

preaching based on performance theory.[20] He understood Scripture as God's self-performance and preaching as an extension of the Word that continues to speak and perform in our world.

This smattering of works exemplifies some of the core ideas and beliefs behind the New Homiletic.[21] The New Homiletic campaigns for the experience of individuals; the uniqueness of listeners' processing patterns; the perception of truth as contextualized, local, and particular; and the emphasis on poetic and artistic expressions in preaching. In short, the New Homiletic may be described as an aggregation of preaching models that diverge from traditional preaching and turn to "homiletical patterns and convictions that had been abandoned or marginalized by modernity."[22] This "turn" refers to (1) the move toward the listener (i.e., hearers are viewed not as passive recipients but as participants who cocreate the experience of the sermon as event); (2) the preference for inductive and narrative sermon forms (i.e., instead of deductive sermons that lay out what people should believe, hearers are invited to appropriate the sermon for their own lives); and (3) the embrace of language as "reality-shaping" (i.e., words do not simply "say" things; they "do" things by shaping human perception and experience).[23]

Conversational Preaching

Among an explosive array of preaching models birthed by the New Homiletic, one of the most interesting—and even the most polarizing—is the

---

20. Charles L. Bartow, *God's Human Speech: A Practical Theology of Proclamation* (Grand Rapids: Eerdmans, 1997).

21. Not listed in this quick sketch are confessional preaching models (e.g., Anna Carter Florence and David Lose), ethnic preaching models (e.g., Henry H. Mitchell, Eunjoo Mary Kim, and Justo González), and contextual preaching models (e.g., Joseph R. Jeter Jr. and Ronald J. Allen; James R. Nieman and Thomas G. Rogers). Eugene Lowry provides a concise overview of these changes in the field of homiletics in the first chapter of his *The Sermon: Dancing the Edge of Mystery* (Nashville: Abingdon, 1997). Richard Eslinger also writes extensively on the diverse preaching styles of the New Homiletic: see *A New Hearing: Living Options in Homiletic Methods* (Nashville: Abingdon, 1987) and *The Web of Preaching: New Options in Homiletic Method* (Nashville: Abingdon, 2002). Eslinger's second book, a sequal fifteen years after his first volume, covers newer ground in homiletics. A helpful critique of the New Homiletic and a discussion of its potential weaknesses can also be found in Charles Campbell's *Preaching Jesus*.

22. Lowry, *Sermon*, 21.

23. O. Wesley Allen Jr., *The Renewed Homiletic* (Minneapolis: Fortress, 2010), 8–9.

conversational homiletic.[24] Strictly speaking, the term *conversational* as it is used here and in recent homiletical literature does not refer to a dialogical style of communication but has to do with a new theological conception of the nature and purpose of preaching.[25] Namely, preaching is considered a shared ministry of people who gather around Scripture to make sense of what God's Word means today to individuals and to a community of believers.

Conversational preaching is not a recent phenomenon or merely a product of the New Homiletic. The conversational model has been profoundly impacted by various preaching traditions and styles across time and denominational lines. According to D. Stephenson Bond, black preaching, Quaker preaching, and the tradition of the Great Awakening testimonials are examples of "seeds" that supply the conversational model with essential theological building blocks. Conversational preaching inherits from black preaching the belief that the sermon is a relational, transactional experience between the preacher and the congregation, one marked by mutual trust and amity, which results in unity and solidarity. In this interactive relationship, the preacher is usually a member of the community who is familiar with the group's story, heritage, and culture and thus speaks as kin or as an empathetic friend who shares their experiences and concerns. The genetic cues from Quaker preaching include the assumption that direct, personal religious experience of God is available to anyone who is attentive to the Spirit. Like an open dialogue among friends who freely affirm, push back, and challenge one another, the sermon is an honest conversation about one's inward consciousness of God—a conversation that involves the community, who is invited to help discern the "inner light"

24. The term *conversational preaching* (most commonly used by Lucy Rose) may also be referred to as *collaborative preaching* (so John McClure) or *ecclesiological conversational homiletic* (so O. Wesley Allen Jr.) in homiletical literature. It should be noted that these labels stand for different viewpoints and emphases, but all three scholars share the conviction that the preacher does not have a monopoly on interpretation and needs others to understand what Scripture means today.

25. O. Wesley Allen Jr. categorizes *conversational preaching* into three broad groups: (1) conversations during the sermon, (2) conversations before the sermon, and (3) sermons with dialogical principles as a foundation. John McClure's collaborative model, which is explored later in this chapter, is an example of the second category, and the works of Rose and Allen are examples of the third group. See O. Wesley Allen Jr., *The Homiletic of All Believers: A Conversational Approach* (Louisville: Westminster John Knox, 2005), 6–14.

and the work of the Spirit. Similarly, the tradition of the Great Awakening testimonials passes on to conversational preaching the fundamental conviction that all believers are equal. All people have a right to share their personal reflections and experiences of God. For this reason, language that fits the pulpit is confessional and autobiographical, not evaluative and authoritative.[26]

Aside from these seeds, the prototypes for today's conversational model are the dialogical sermons birthed out of the homiletical experimentations in the 1960s and '70s.[27] The homiletical precursors from that period include Bernard Lee's "shared homily," which encourages a real dialogue between the minister and members of the congregation during worship;[28] Dietrich Ritschl's and Browne Barr's pre-sermon Bible discussions, which involve the whole church as active learners and contributors to shaping the sermon;[29] and Reuel Howe's and George A. Swank's advocating that the sermon's function is to shape the church's conversations through Scripture by enabling the members to think for themselves and arrive at their own conclusions about what the text means and how it applies to their lives.[30] As we move on to examine the more recent conversational preaching models by Lucy Rose, John McClure, and O. Wesley Allen Jr., it is important to see their works as building on the ideas and convictions of their predecessors and friends in kindred traditions.

Lucy Rose: Conversational Preaching[31]

Lucy Rose's homiletic model rests on two preliminary convictions: (1) the need for partnership between preachers and congregations, and

26. For more on these three traditions, refer to D. Stephenson Bond, *Interactive Preaching* (St. Louis: Chalice, 1991), 54–72.

27. Allen, *Homiletic of All Believers*, 6.

28. Bernard J. Lee, "Shared Homily: Conversation That Puts Communities at Risk," in *Alternative Futures for Worship: The Eucharist*, ed. Bernard J. Lee (Collegeville, MN: Liturgical Press, 1987).

29. See Dietrich Ritschl, *A Theology of Preaching* (Richmond: John Knox, 1960), and Browne Barr, *Parish Talk Back* (Nashville: Abingdon, 1964).

30. See Reuel Howe, *Partners in Preaching: Clergy and Laity in Dialogue* (New York: Seabury Press, 1967), and George Swank, *Dialogic Style in Preaching* (Valley Forge, PA: Judson Press, 1981).

31. Lucy Atkinson Rose died at the age of fifty in 1997 after a four-year struggle with cancer, but her legacy as a scholar is profound in the homiletical field. Fellow homiletician David Lose comments that "few, if any, homileticians have given greater attention to the hearer's role

(2) the view that all language is limited, biased, and, ultimately, "fallen."[32] These convictions stem from her dissatisfaction with approaches to preaching that tend to treat the minister as an answer-person who unleashes Scripture's meaning and power to the congregation by facilitating a life-changing encounter with God through the sermon.[33] Such a view promotes a hazardous understanding of preaching on a number of levels. For one, it gives the false impression that the sermon is a ubiquitous answer to life's manifold problems without regard to context and that the preacher is responsible for providing that answer. Also, these expectations unrealistically inflate the sermon such that a single preaching event is forced to bear the full burden of a person's transformation. Furthermore, the view of preaching that unduly emphasizes the change in an individual or the individual's situation threatens to undermine the communal identity of the church. Worship ceases to be a formative communal activity and is instead reduced to a privatized event that nurtures self-absorbed consumerism and self-idolatry. In addition to the degradation of worship, it also reduces the congregation to passive recipients. The preacher becomes the sole arbiter of truth, with the congregation fully dependent on the preacher to hear and discern what God is saying to them. According to Rose, the destructive power imbalance between the preacher and the congregation is caused and sustained by the view of language as a neutral, value-free medium of communication. Many in the church have unwittingly and unsuspectingly accepted that language conveys the objective reality of the world without historical conditioning and untainted by the preacher's

---

in contemporary preaching than Lucy Atkinson Rose" (David Lose, *Confessing Jesus Christ: Preaching in a Postmodern World* [Grand Rapids: Eerdmans, 2003], 126). Rose's best-known publications are *Sharing the Word: Preaching in the Roundtable Church* (Louisville: Westminster John Knox, 1997) and *Songs in the Night: A Witness to God's Love in Life and in Death* (Decatur, GA: CTS Press, 1998). Of these, this discussion will explore the former, which most clearly outlines the conversational model.

32. Rose, *Sharing the Word*, 81, 89–91.

33. Rose names three prominent theories of preaching: (1) traditional theory, which extends the Augustinian legacy of preaching as a "sacred rhetoric" that conjoins Christian preaching and classical rhetoric; (2) kerygmatic theory, which is influenced by the ideas of C. H. Dodd that stress the transmission of the *kerygma* in preaching; and (3) transformational theory, which emphasizes listeners' transcendent experience of the sermon. The first two categories of her classification more or less correspond to what this work refers to broadly as the *traditional homiletic*. The third category relates to preaching models birthed by the New Homiletic, such as those surveyed at the beginning of this chapter.

personal assumptions, prejudices, and blind spots. Language has come to be regarded as an unbiased tool that the preacher freely wields to produce calculated change in listeners.

Rose confronts these long-held assumptions and patterns of the pulpit, speaking out against the inequality between the preacher and the congregation and the understanding of language as a clear, unpolluted channel of communication. To her, the sermon is "where the central conversations of the church are fostered and refocused week after week." Rejecting the traditional hierarchy, the conversational model treats the preacher and the congregation as equal partners—like colleagues who "gather symbolically at a roundtable without head or foot."[34] This egalitarian vision of preaching sees the church as a hospitable community that thrives by making room for diverse interpretations and experiences in the ongoing conversations about Christian life. The preacher does not "[impede] these conversations with a final or single answer . . . [but] fosters the conversations of the church by explicitly acknowledging a variety of points of view, learning processes, interpretations, and life experiences."[35] She suggests that "connectedness" and "mutuality" be the preacher's mode of relating to the congregation. Solidarity begins with the church, the family of believers, but ultimately it must extend to the margins of the world, where "the church and the world become connected as a circle of friends."[36]

Rose contends that "all language, including the language of faith, is inevitably biased and limited, historically conditioned, and inseparable from the sins of each generation and each community of users."[37] That being so, we cannot really know truth because truth can be spoken of only eschatologically, when all things will be revealed one day.[38] On this side of heaven, then, preaching aims to inspire "conversations that *all* contribute to the formation and reformation of God's people on our way toward the eschaton where we believe and hope we will see God face-to-face."[39]

---

34. Rose, *Sharing the Word*, 4.
35. Rose, *Sharing the Word*, 96.
36. Letty M. Russell, *Church in the Round: Feminist Interpretation of the Church* (Louisville: Westminster John Knox, 1993), 19, quoted in Rose, *Sharing the Word*, 122.
37. Rose, *Sharing the Word*, 90.
38. Rose, *Sharing the Word*, 5.
39. Rose, *Sharing the Word*, 6.

Through preaching, the whole church leans in to participate in a lively discussion that approximates truth by considering diverse perspectives.

Rose therefore defines preaching as a tentative interpretation of a biblical text and of God's activity in the world as meaning that makes life bearable and worthwhile. It is a proposal that creates space for genuine conversation, invites counterproposals, and fosters mutual encouragement, edification, and sometimes transformation among all the participants in the church's central conversations. It is a wager on the part of the preacher, a genuine yet humble confession of faith that acknowledges its particularity and self-interest and seeks the corrective and confirmation of the wagers of others.[40]

The kind of language fit for communal preaching is "confessional" (i.e., "reflecting the accumulated and the ongoing experiences of the people of God") and "evocative" (i.e., "able to generate multiple meanings"). "Confessional" implies (1) acknowledging the convictions, positions, and viewpoints of the religious community that shape the preacher's interpretation of God's Word, and (2) acknowledging the preacher's personal convictions.[41] Maintaining these two senses, Rose argues that the focus of preaching must "[shift] from truth as an external reality to truth as an experience."[42] Rather than seeing language as an instrument of persuasion that establishes what is normative and universal, the confessional language of conversational preaching "belongs to the community of faith, and evocative language invites those gathered to participate in the community's ongoing, central conversations."[43] The form of the conversational sermon should reflect the preacher's inner journey toward meaning and be open-ended enough to allow other voices to interact with the sermon in their own ways.

John McClure: Collaborative Preaching[44]

The question that lies at the heart of John McClure's homiletical proposal is this: How can preaching help shape faith communities to be truly

40. Rose, *Sharing the Word*, 107.
41. Rose, *Sharing the Word*, 108–9.
42. Rose, *Sharing the Word*, 109.
43. Rose, *Sharing the Word*, 110.
44. John McClure is a minister and homiletician with interests in philosophy, theology, ethics, and culture. Much of what is presented in this section comes from his book *The Roundtable Pulpit*. His prolific contributions to preaching include *The Four Codes of Preaching: Rhetorical Strategies* (Louisville: Westminster John Knox, 2003); *The Roundtable Pulpit: Where Preaching*

countercultural in our troubled world? For preaching to have a transformative influence, McClure believes that sermons must do more than teach;
preaching needs to be an exercise in *collaborative* leadership that empowers the laity to live as fully committed disciples of Christ. Collaborative or
consultative leadership is effective in building unified communities with
strong lay commitment, especially in situations that demand high personal
or institutional risks from members.[45] When members have an acute sense
of ownership and responsibility for the communities they are part of, they
are more willing to sacrificially give themselves and their resources for a
common cause.

McClure draws attention to two interconnected aspects of collaborative
leadership that preachers need to keep in mind. The first is "integrative
power," which is "the way a leader connects the narrow concerns within
the community with other communities and with the public interest at
large." The second is "nutritive power," which refers to "the way a leader
includes followers in an active role as interpreters of their situation and as
decision makers about their own future." Empowering people is not the
end of preaching but a means of helping people live out public theology
that "reconnects the gospel message with the public realm."[46] The public
sphere is where "strangers" can be encountered—"the mysterious presence of something which contests [our] projecting meaning on it."[47] Here,
McClure uses the term *stranger* to refer both to God, who is the *Holy*

---

and Leadership Meet (Nashville: Abingdon, 1995); *Best Advice for Preaching* (Minneapolis:
Fortress, 1998); *Other-Wise Preaching: A Postmodern Ethic for Homiletics* (St. Louis: Chalice,
2001); *Preaching Words: 144 Key Terms in Homiletics* (Louisville: Westminster John Knox,
2007); *Mashup Religion: Pop Music and Theological Intervention* (Waco: Baylor University
Press, 2011); John McClure and Nancy Ramsey, eds., *Telling the Truth: Preaching about
Sexual and Domestic Violence* (Cleveland: United Church Press, 1998); and John McClure
and Burton Z. Cooper, *Claiming Theology in the Pulpit* (Louisville: Westminster John Knox,
2003). *The Roundtable Pulpit* lays out McClure's collaborative model most clearly in practical terms, including its benefits and methodology. For a more in-depth look at his theology
of preaching (vis-à-vis the theology of the Other), refer to *Other-Wise Preaching*, in which
McClure sets a larger backdrop of philosophical and homiletical shifts that influence his
perspective on preaching. He also provides a more in-depth look at the convictions that guide
his homiletic theology. I have used these two books here because they provide the clearest
delineation of McClure's ideas for a collaborative (conversational) preaching model and his
methodology for executing it.

45. McClure, *Roundtable Pulpit*, 12.
46. McClure, *Roundtable Pulpit*, 13.
47. Edward Farley, *Good and Evil: Interpreting a Human Condition* (Minneapolis: Augsburg
Fortress, 1992), 8–9, quoted in McClure, *Roundtable Pulpit*, 14.

Other, and to *human* others. These two aspects of collaborative leadership address the danger that the traditional homiletic can inadvertently violate the otherness of God and our neighbors.[48] On the one hand, the otherness of God is violated when preachers fail to consider the congregation's diverse perspectives on Scripture. When preachers "preclude new information and arguments that represent contrary positions" and instead "[rehash] or [repeat] older, timeworn messages," the church misses out on the full range of what the Scriptures might be saying today.[49] On the other hand, preaching violates human neighbors when preachers uphold a centralized view of authority that elevates themselves as the revealer of divine mandates over the congregation, who must accept and obey them as passive recipients. A hierarchical preaching style that does not treat members as agent-subjects erodes the listeners' faith, experience, and identity as the people of God.

Pastors who preach inductive and narrative sermons have made recent efforts to pay closer attention to listeners. Even though this effort is laudable, McClure regrets that these approaches do not inspire a mutual form of persuasion between the preacher and the congregation.[50] In these models, preachers act as storytellers who journey alongside listeners to explore the meaning and significance of God's Word. At first glance, this seems like a step in a positive direction that establishes relational symmetry between the preacher and the congregation. In reality, however, what appears as a thrilling narrative expedition filled with surprises and self-discoveries only has one predetermined path that leads to a clear destination designated by the preacher. Also problematic in inductive and narrative preaching is the emphasis on a shared narrative experience and the assumed similarity between the preacher and the congregation, which downplay the real differences between people and enforce an artificial uniformity.[51] Another danger of these preaching models is individualism bred by an overt focus on a personal experience of the sermon, which impedes the cultivation of a genuinely unified Christian community.[52]

48. McClure, *Roundtable Pulpit*, 30–38.
49. McClure, *Roundtable Pulpit*, 37.
50. McClure, *Roundtable Pulpit*, 39–47.
51. McClure, *Roundtable Pulpit*, 42–43.
52. McClure, *Roundtable Pulpit*, 43–44.

In light of the insufficiencies of existing preaching models and the
changes brought on by postmodernism and its skepticism toward established authorities, McClure urges minsters to rethink preaching. He suggests that preaching needs to "deconstruct" existing texts by exposing
hidden assumptions, latent claims to authority, and disillusionment about
a stable meaning.[53] The purpose of challenging the established notions
of power, experience, and understanding that constitute a tradition is to
expand our inclusion of *others* instead of bending the knee to the idol of
the social status quo. McClure refers to this centrifugal and other-oriented
preaching as "other-wise homiletics." He writes, "Other-wise homiletics
is homiletics that is, in every aspect, other-inspired and other-directed. It
is homiletics that strives to become wise about other human beings—to
gain wisdom about and from others for preaching. At the same time, it
is homiletics that . . . becomes patently other-wise than homiletics itself,
that is, it seeks to place the totality of homiletics under deconstructive
erasure so that preaching might be transformed by a profound awareness
of the proximity of preaching's 'others.'"[54]

In order to practice preaching that is truly other oriented, McClure
contends that preachers must deconstruct and "exit" four "houses" that
have long functioned as authorities for the church's understanding of
preaching: Scripture, tradition, experience, and reason.[55] By exiting the
house of Scripture, preachers discover that the nature of the Bible is
to de-center and dislocate the positions and identities that Christians
generally cling to as expressions of their mastery over Scripture. This
form of erasure breaks down the established rules and patterns of the
language game that Christians play and allows us to draw closer to God
and human others.

Exiting the house of tradition allows preachers to use countermemory
to remember people on the margins who have been harmed or excluded
from the church's official memory, which forms a tradition. When preachers undergo this shift, they realize that their role is not as safekeepers who
guard the treasures of old but as shepherds who must search out and care
for the hurt.

---

53. McClure, *Other-Wise Preaching*, 1–12.
54. McClure, *Other-Wise Preaching*, xi.
55. McClure, *Other-Wise Preaching*, 2.

As preachers exit the house of experience, they gain awareness of the illusory nature of what is "universal" and "common" about human experience. When preachers reject the naive assumption that undisputed objectivity exists for all people, they can then start paying attention to the specific struggles, pain, and joys of real people. In this turn to strangers, ministers can look beyond "normative" human or ecclesial experience that has long functioned as the basis of authority in preaching and begin to celebrate the glory of God glimpsed in real people.

Finally, exiting the house of reason enables preachers to overcome the long-standing dichotomy between faith and reason that has marked the Western church. Moving away from representational epistemology that springs from scientific positivism and propositional-deductive homiletics, McClure invites pastors to embrace preaching that is confessional and testimonial.

In the spirit of other-wise preaching, McClure proposes a collaborative homiletic in which laity and clergy share leadership in biblical interpretation. In his work *The Roundtable Pulpit*, he suggests that the preacher and the congregation gather before the sermon to engage in a "face-to-face," "participatory," and "interactive persuasion" as they collectively discern the Word for their particular congregation.[56] The symbolic roundtable of these "human strangers"[57] reflects the community's actual perspectives and responses to encountering Scripture. As different or as similar as they may be, everyone is welcome to come as they are and bring their unique stories and gifts to engage one another in an ongoing exploration of Scripture. McClure views God's Word as an emergent Word—a communal Word that must be interpreted by the ecclesial body as members "come to terms" with it.[58] "Coming to terms" does not mean reaching a consensus on meaning but rather indicates "a quality of relationships" between members as they "decide on ways to stand *with* and stand *for*

56. McClure, *Roundtable Pulpit*, 20–25.
57. McClure quotes Patrick R. Keifer in explaining that "human strangers" are (1) those who are outside of the church, (2) "inside strangers who remain outside the intimate group that usually makes up most of the leadership in a congregation," and (3) "the irreducible difference between two persons that exists in any encounter." Patrick R. Keifer, *Welcoming the Stranger: A Public Theology of Worship and Evangelism* (Minneapolis: Fortress, 1992), 8–9, quoted in McClure, *Other-Wise Preaching*, 14.
58. McClure, *Roundtable Pulpit*, 23.

one another by claiming tentative *directions* of thought and actions as God's Word."[59] The preacher's role in this table fellowship is as a hospitable host who facilitates an honest and open conversation instead of manipulating or controlling to achieve a desired outcome. At the same time, the preacher also has a responsibility to act as a "steward of both the story of Christ and the tradition of the community . . . see[ing] to it that all conversations and sacramental actions are centered on the saving work of Jesus Christ and on the mission of the church."[60]

The roundtable pre-sermon meeting should take place weekly and involve no more than ten pre-selected, rotating members of the congregation. In a segmented ninety-minute session, the group should discuss the following:

Feedback/feedforward (10 mins.)
   The cohost allows the group to talk about how the previous week's roundtable discussion and sermon relate to this week's conversation.
Engaging the biblical text (20 mins.)
   The preacher seeks to "make Scripture an active 'voice' at the roundtable"[61] by sharing historical and literary background of the text. Although the preacher is a central voice that guides the discussion so that the text is not misconstrued, the group must be allowed to freely interpret and interact with the text.
Engaging one another (60 mins.)
   In this segment, the participants "lift their heads out of the biblical text and engage one another in a conversation about their own insights, questions, experiences, and issues. This is the portion of the sermon roundtable that will be most important for the development of [the] sermon."[62]

How does the roundtable conversation bear on the sermon? Collaborative preaching takes the form of a monological sermon that is dialogical in content. In other words, the minister may stand at the pulpit alone,

59. McClure, *Roundtable Pulpit*, 24.
60. McClure, *Roundtable Pulpit*, 29.
61. McClure, *Roundtable Pulpit*, 67.
62. McClure, *Roundtable Pulpit*, 67.

but the sermon itself resounds many interpretive voices that have taken part in shaping it. The role of the sermon is to report the *dynamics* of the conversation by *describing* or *imitating* essential elements of the group experience.[63] The hope is that "all may hear the variety of ways in which the congregation is coming to terms with the gospel of Jesus Christ."[64]

O. Wesley Allen Jr.: Ecclesiological Preaching[65]

O. Wesley Allen Jr. observes the pervasiveness of cultural postmodernism in *The Homiletic of All Believers*. Many today tend to view truth as particular, local, and relative, and reject the notion of a metanarrative undergirded by absolute truth. As the glory days of the Enlightenment, which crowned objectivity and reason as the be-all answers to life, are fading, Allen believes that people are more interested in *meaning-making* rather than searching for a stable, universal meaning. In such a transitional time as this, the church faces this predicament: "How is the church to proclaim the gospel when those in the pews are likely to be suspicious of any authoritative claims preachers (or anyone else) make? How are we to preach to a gathering of hearers who are not seeking meaning from us, but are at best going about the task of making meaning for themselves and who approach the Christian faith and what preachers have to say about and from it as one resource among many?" The church has two choices: to take a stand against postmodernism and not engage the culture or to seriously grapple with the epistemological shifts and the newly rising concerns and pursue a creative approach to preaching that "allows preachers both to remain faithful to the ancient Christian traditions

63. McClure, *Roundtable Pulpit*, 73.
64. McClure, *Roundtable Pulpit*, 58.
65. As a scholar-minister whose interests include worship, preaching, and the interpretation of the New Testament, O. Wesley Allen Jr. has contributed much to scholarship through publications including *Good News from Tinyville: Stories of Heart and Hope* (St. Louis: Chalice, 1999); *Interpreting the Synoptic Gospels: Basic Methods for Interpreting Matthew, Mark, and Luke* (St. Louis: Chalice, 2000); *Preaching Resurrection* (St. Louis: Chalice, 2000); *The Homiletic of All Believers: A Conversational Approach* (Louisville: Westminster John Knox, 2005); *Preaching and Reading the Lectionary: The Three Dimensions of the Liturgical Year* (St. Louis: Chalice, 2007); and *Determining the Form: Structures for Preaching* (Minneapolis: Fortress, 2008). Among these, Allen's own theology of preaching is most extensively laid out in *The Homiletic of All Believers*. For this reason, this work will be the primary source for examining Allen's conversational/ecclesiological homiletic.

and to embrace postmodern congregations."[66] Allen chooses the latter
and submits what he calls "conversational" or "ecclesial" homiletic as a
solution.

His homiletical model is built on two foundational convictions: (1) "a
view of the church as a community of theological, political, historical,
spiritual, ritual, and existential conversation," and (2) "a view of preaching
in which the pulpit is placed on the edge of the community's conversational
circle and the preacher's is one voice among many in a matrix of congregational conversations."[67] In order to accommodate the postmoderns who
make meaning in a conversational manner—"giving and taking from the
myriad of 'conversation' partners we have in today's world"—he suggests
that preachers view the congregation not as recipients of religious meaning but as providers of it.[68] Following the theology of the priesthood of
all believers, Allen calls for *the homiletic of all believers*.

An ecclesial homiletic begins in an open-ended interaction where the
preacher and the congregation practice the conversational ethics of mutual
trust, an egalitarian view of one another as subjects in conversation (not as
objects to be persuaded), reciprocity of respect, and acceptance of asym-
metry of beliefs and experience (openness to differences in perspectives
and convictions).[69] The goal of the interaction is for "all conversational
participants to be converted in the sense of growing in their understanding,
relationship to, and interaction with God, self, and the world in light of
Christian traditions, and . . . [for] the conversational community to be
transformed by both the tensions and the mutual understandings that
occur in the process of conversing."[70]

A dialogical and egalitarian vision of preaching considers the ministry
of the Word alongside other ministries of the church. The sermon "ceases
to be the starting point or the center of the conversation and becomes a
significant contributing factor to the ongoing conversations owned by the
community."[71] Likewise, the preacher is one among many conversation
partners. Since the presence of authority is inevitable in any educational

66. Allen, *Homiletic of All Believers*, 5.
67. Allen, *Homiletic of All Believers*, 16.
68. Allen, *Homiletic of All Believers*, 17.
69. Allen, *Homiletic of All Believers*, 25–27.
70. Allen, *Homiletic of All Believers*, 31.
71. Allen, *Homiletic of All Believers*, 15.

endeavor, Allen acknowledges that the preacher has a "privileged voice."[72] What matters, however, is neither the presence nor the absence of authority but *where* the pulpit is placed in the community of faith. Are the pulpit and the preacher "actively participating in the congregation's conversation circles by offering a specialized voice in the give-and-take proclamation of the church"?[73]

The modern paradigm has caused theology to be professionalized, and as a result, congregations often fail to see God's pervasive presence in the world. So the sermon's purpose is to name and "piece together"[74] God's constant presence in every facet of our lives and, being attuned to this reality, to invite people to make meaning of their lives and the world. In this sense, sermons are analogous to "vocabulary lessons" in which the preacher as a "language teacher" teaches theologically illiterate congregations the language of Christian traditions so that they can describe and shape reality in light of who God is.[75] Allen believes that when the language of the congregation changes, so does the culture of the community.

Allen imagines preachers as being like photographers who "through their homiletical cameras . . . artistically offer new perspectives of what the congregation has been looking at all along" but has missed or failed to see. In a way, any member of the faith community can take on this role. The only difference between ministers and lay members "lies in the training and equipment that preachers bring with them to the task of offering proclamatory snapshots of God's presence in the world."[76] Employing a wide range of tools from biblical theology, church history, and hermeneutics, preachers develop a "trained eye" that can see God's presence in the ordinary and in the not-so-ordinary affairs of life (e.g., disaster, suffering, other problems of evil). As preachers engage the congregation's diverse matrix of conversations, Allen recommends that they consider six homiletical contexts in particular: personal (i.e., the preacher's own pre-understandings and presuppositions), congregational (i.e., the ethos of the community), theological (i.e., systematic theology and history of

72. Allen, *Homiletic of All Believers*, 39.
73. Allen, *Homiletic of All Believers*, 40.
74. Allen, *Homiletic of All Believers*, 45.
75. Allen, *Homiletic of All Believers*, 53–57.
76. Allen, *Homiletic of All Believers*, 45.

Table 2.1: Summary of Rose's, McClure's, and Allen's Preaching Models

Homiletician	Lucy Rose	John McClure	O. Wesley Allen Jr.
Preaching Model	Conversational preaching	Collaborative preaching	Ecclesiological homiletic
Description	The sermon serves greater conversations of the church.	Pre-sermon conversations serve the sermon.	The preaching ministry (not a single sermon) serves congregational conversations.
Focus	A theology of conversational preaching To address the deficiencies of other homiletical models, in particular with regard to the preacher's authority and view of language (focuses on the "what" and the "why" of preaching rather than the "how")	"Centrifugal" preaching that focuses on others To welcome laity around a sermon roundtable in order to empower them as leaders	Homiletical ecclesiology and ecclesiological homiletic To understand the whole of preaching ministry as a way of assisting people to engage in conversations about God. Preaching is one of many ministries that serve the congregation's ongoing proclamations of the gospel
Preacher	A member of the community / facilitator of conversation who puts forth one interpretation	A host who exercises temporal inequality of authority at the time of preaching	A specialist who has some authority to share expertise that aids the conversation
Sermon	Tentative interpretation, proposal, wager	A report of conversational dynamics	Vocabulary lessons that supply Christian language toward meaning-making
Sermonic Form	Inductive/narrative and story forms preferred Open to any form that is testimonial and evokes a multiplicity of meanings that encourage mutual exchange	Inductive form with attention to the conversational dynamics of pre-sermon roundtable discussion	A variety of forms can be used in the sermonic conversation, just as real-life conversations employ many literary forms

doctrine), sociohistorical (i.e., events of the community, country, world),
liturgical (i.e., the worship context), and conversational (i.e., the matrix
of all conversational circles occurring within the congregation).[77]

Conclusion: Points of Contact between the Three Models

Distilling the similarities between the three models is trickier than it may
seem. Although all three scholars draw from a broad range of homiletical and theological literature, each proponent offers a unique take on
what it might mean for preaching to be a shared ministry of the church.
Relying on feminist scholarship, philosophical linguistics, and liberation
theology, Rose's main contribution is in aiding preachers to reconsider the
theology of popular approaches to preaching and in shedding light on the
prevailing views of authority and language. Her answer to a hierarchical
understanding of the preacher's authority and a debasing perception of
language is the conversational homiletic.

McClure's collaborative homiletic focuses on how preaching serves to
empower the laity. He draws heavily on philosophical and theological
literature, as well as leadership studies. With special interest in theology
as a public act, McClure grounds his ideas in deconstructionism and, in
particular, in the work of Emmanuel Levinas relating to the concept of
other. Preaching, as McClure portrays it, has a centrifugal quality that
refuses closure on Scripture, tradition, experience, and reason; instead, it
opens up new and fresh conversations that constantly orient the church
toward the margins.

Allen, however, bases his thoughts largely on sociological and pedagogical literature. To him, preaching is one of many meaning-making conversations in the church that try to make sense of our identity and calling
as Christians. Unlike Rose and McClure, Allen's major contribution is
offering a practical picture of what a conversational preaching ministry
might look like in the week-to-week life of a church.

Despite the disparities among the works of Rose, McClure, and Allen,
similarities can also be gleaned. First, their works point to and embody the
cultural shift from an overarching, grand narrative to "smaller" stories of

77. Allen, *Homiletic of All Believers*, 46–49.

individuals and subcultures. Without an unquestionable epistemological foundation, context is key in today's culture: people interpret texts from their own social location, inescapably colored by a miscellany of experiences that fashion their attitudes and perspectives. Knowledge claims are considered social constructions that say more about us as knowing subjects (why do we think the way we do?). So the fragmentation of knowledge requires interaction within the community of other knowers. Understanding, growth, and even transformation become possible through mutual sharing. Preaching is not a didactic endeavor that unilaterally passes on knowledge to listeners. The conversational scholars urge preachers to relinquish the traditional search for an all-encompassing meaning and to think of the sermon as a fluid, provisional communal sharing.

Second, the preeminence of reason and objectivity that guides traditional preaching gives way to the preference for experience and subjectivity in the preaching models of Rose, McClure, and Allen. Since there is no totalizing reason, these preachers reject absolutism and consider truth elusive and something that can only be approximated. They favor the language of confession and testimony over universal propositions and assertions because matters of faith are best communicated metaphorically and poetically by considering diverse points of view. It is in the eclectic collection of fragmented stories and perspectives that the church glimpses something of God's mysterious *otherness*. The conversational ethic values an endless play of communal exploration with and about God that takes us beyond our situated knowledge rather than to the finality of arriving at fixed conclusions.

Third, the conversational model decentralizes the pulpit and translocates it to the margins of the church and society. The conversational scholars believe that words are more than a medium for expressing thoughts and feelings because language has the power to shape social consciousness. Yet they consider language that is rooted and influenced by cultural ideology to be tainted by the world's dynamics of power relations. This makes all language faulty and untrustworthy, including preaching. In the name of God, the Bible, and Christian tradition, the pulpit has served, and still often does serve, the interests of those in positions of influence. Protesting against the pulpit's role in legitimizing hegemony, the conversational scholars cry out for the equality and solidarity of preachers with the rest of the church. Their homiletical proposals are pleas for the inclusion of all who have been traditionally marginalized by the systemic injustices sustained in our language. Their hope is for preaching to stimulate honest conversations throughout the church about the often-concealed themes of power relations and, by doing so, for the pulpit to become a model of Christian hospitality and love in the public realm.

The similarities in the thoughts and underlying themes of Rose, McClure, and Allen characterize the postmodern ethos. *Postmodernism* is a notoriously sticky word, denoting myriad philosophical and cultural orientations in a wide range of disciplines, such as art, architecture, literature, science, philosophy, and history. Although its diffusiveness makes postmodernism a challenge to define, it is not without conspicuous traits, such as "an epistemological shift in our approach to truth; a decline in absolutism and an increase in perspectivalism (the idea that claims to truth are mostly a matter of point of view); a decrease in confidence in reason and our ability to know objective reality; and a corresponding emphasis on relationships, affective responses, and the importance of community and tradition."[78] The following chapter examines some of these traits that distill the postmodern ethos. The goal of the next chapter is to assess the claims of the conversational homiletic from the bottom up by understanding the operating assumptions and values of postmodernism.

---

78. Dennis M. Cahill borrows from the ideas of D. A. Carson in *Becoming Conversant with the Emerging Church: Understanding a Movement and Its Implications* (Grand Rapids: · Zondervan, 2005). See Dennis M. Cahill, *The Shape of Preaching: Theory and Practice in Sermon Design* (Grand Rapids: Baker Books, 2007), 69; see also 75.

3

A Critique of the
Conversational Homiletic

The past several decades of Western scholarship can be described as a whirlwind of delineation, evaluation, and adaptation that are due to the multifaceted changes associated with postmodernism. David Lose describes the postmodern turn as having "irrevocably altered our intellectual landscape."[1] If Lose is right, then preachers today live at a critical time that requires thoughtful reflection on the changes society has undergone and continues to experience. The exact nature of postmodernism—whether it is an implosion, rupture, transition, or aftermath of modernity—is perhaps best left to debate. With regard to this chapter, however, we need to identify key traits of this era that imbue the conversational homiletic.[2] The goal of this chapter is to understand

1. David J. Lose, *Confessing Jesus Christ: Preaching in a Postmodern World* (Grand Rapids: Eerdmans, 2003), 1.
2. Two points of clarification may be helpful. First, postmodernism defies a single definition because it refers to a wide range of philosophical stances and aesthetic styles that signal a retreat from the ideas and values of modernism. Notwithstanding its complexity, this section names several stand-out features of postmodernism that distinguish it from the preceding philosophical era. Second, the *postmodern turn* should not, however, be taken to mean a complete discontinuity between the modern and the postmodern worlds or the impossibility of any overlap or coexistence of the two worlds, for the rate of change differs for cultures and social locations. The intent here is neither to homogenize modernity or postmodernity nor to exaggerate their differences but to name the dominant themes of the respective epistemologies experienced at different rates by different cultures and social spheres.

the current epistemological milieu that gave birth to the conversational homiletic and, from there, to critique the principles, assumptions, and values inherent to conversational preaching.

Six Traits of the Postmodern Turn

Practice-Oriented Approach

Postmodernism represents a shift from a *theory-centered philosophy* to a *practice-oriented approach*. Aristotle once identified three modes of "being" that depict how human beings engage the world they live in: *theoria* (the domain of theoretical/scientific knowledge), *praxis* (the domain of practical/political knowledge), and *poiesis* (the domain of creative/ productive knowledge). However, after Aristotle the concepts of *praxis* and *poiesis* began to fade from the thoughts of Western philosophy, and only *theoria* remained as the superior way of life that ensures the certainty of knowledge (consider especially the Enlightenment). Theory occupied a high place in academia, being crowned as "the darling of ancients and moderns alike." The ancient Greeks equated *theoria* with "the eternal truths that one beholds with the mind's eye," and the moderns considered it "the product of universal reason or the scientific method [that] has unmatched explanatory power."[3]

A world governed by theoretical and scientific knowledge treated practical and creative knowledge like second-class citizens. This was also true of practical theology as a discipline, which included preaching. For the greater part of Christian history, a wide chasm separated theory and practice in the study of theology. In fact, theology itself was divided into two hierarchical parts: systematic theology (theology "proper"), which was valued as the crux of the whole discipline, and practical theology, its subordinate and derivative.

The inherent hierarchy in the degradation of *praxis* and *poiesis* in favor of *theoria* could be seen in how a theological inquiry began: the theoretical inquiry came first and was followed by practice or application. What mattered the most in theological studies was theoretical

3. Kevin J. Vanhoozer, *The Drama of Doctrine: A Canonical Linguistic Approach to Christian Theology* (Louisville: Westminster John Knox, 2005), 13.

reflection, and the "action" of how those reflections were translated into everyday living as skills and habits was less essential. Describing this kind of approach to theology as being "Barthian" in essence, Don Browning states, "A theologian as recent as Karl Barth saw theology as the systematic interpretation of God's self-disclosure to the Christian church. There was no role for human understanding, action, or practice in the construal of God's self-disclosure. In this view, theology is practical only by applying God's revelation as directly and purely as possible to the concrete situations of life. The theologian moves from revealed knowledge to application."[4]

In past decades, however, the discipline of theology has undergone a makeover of sorts by reinstalling *praxis* and *poiesis* to their rightful places. Doubt has been cast over the legitimacy of the old prevailing model of inquiry (which moved from theory to practice) because of a growing recognition that every practice is actually theory laden. Unlike the former portrayal of their relationship, theory and practice are actually inseparable because theories do not emerge out of nowhere; they rise out of praxis and return back to inform the praxis (hence the *practice-theory-practice model*).[5] The shift from a one-directional, linear understanding of the theory and practice relationship to a circular, interrelated paradigm may not sound very significant, but it has had a profound impact on reframing theology as a "theory of action."[6] The church and academy have a revived recognition that theology is practical through and through. Theology arises from the real, concrete needs and experiences of people in diverse contexts, and its goal is to direct practical actions for life.

Focus on Ontology

The result of separating theory and practice in modern thinking is an unnatural separation of *knowing* and *being*. Modernism's penchant for

4. Don S. Browning, *A Fundamental Practical Theology: Descriptive and Strategic Proposals* (Minneapolis: Fortress, 1991), 5.

5. To read more on this topic, see Browning, *Fundamental Practical Theology*; Gerben Heitink, *Practical Theology*, trans. Reinder Bruinsma (Grand Rapids: Eerdmans, 1999); Thomas H. Groome, *Sharing Faith: A Comprehensive Approach to Religious Education and Pastoral Ministry* (Eugene, OR: Wipf & Stock, 1991); Ray S. Anderson, *The Shape of Practical Theology: Empowering Ministry with Theological Praxis* (Downers Grove, IL: InterVarsity Press, 2001).

6. See Heitink, *Practical Theology*.

rationality and certitude enthrones *cognition* (i.e., apprehension through reasoning). This leads to viewing scientific and technological progress as the greatest achievement and promotes the goal of knowing in itself over the more fundamental and integral usefulness of knowledge to shape a person's essential nature. As reason is prioritized and valued over experience, and as theory is lifted above practice, knowledge without agency does not appear senseless or aberrant. Theological education is no exception to this outlook. Inculcating knowledge apart from any transformation in the human agent has become the norm in many pulpits and seminary lecterns. Sallie McFague TeSelle speaks about the result: "If theology becomes overly abstract, conceptual and systematic, it separates thought and life, belief and practice, words and their embodiment."[7]

As a theory-centered approach yields to a practice-oriented approach, however, a shift occurs from *epistemology* to *ontology*, from the enterprise of *knowing* to *knowing-subjects*. The restored focus on ontology redefines the purpose of theology as *conation*—"holistic intent of a knowing/desiring/doing that engages and shapes the whole 'being' of people as agent-subjects in the world."[8] Thomas Groome uses the term *conation* (or *epistemic ontology*) to indicate that the outcome of all Christian ministry (including the work of pastors and theological educators) ought to be lived Christian faith. The aim of Christian ministry is to cause a deep, comprehensive transformation in people. Right knowledge is not a matter of the mind but should take hold of people, permeate their beings, and govern their imaginations, hearts, and attitudes, empowering them to live wisely in the world. If wisdom is seen as the dialectic between Scripture and the contemporary world, then the *telos* of theology is not disseminating information but nurturing biblical wisdom that enables upright living in a changing, turbulent world. The philosophical turn to conation resurrects wisdom (i.e., lived knowledge, embodied knowledge) and makes its cultivation an integral project of theology. Wisdom is seen as that which "more than anything else, enables us to traverse the ugly ditch between theory and practice."[9]

7. Sallie McFague TeSelle, "Parable, Metaphor and Theology," *Journal of the American Academy of Religion* 42, no. 4 (1974): 630.

8. Groome, *Sharing Faith*, 26–27.

9. Vanhoozer, *Drama of Doctrine*, 13.

Recovery of Ethics

The focus on ontology and the restoration of wisdom leads to another important change: *the recovery of ethics*. An unfortunate consequence of modernity's trenchant dualism of the mind and body, reason and experience, and theory and practice has been an enervated conscience without a strong sense of responsibility to live out what we claim to know. In the abnormal state where knowing is divorced from being, knowledge does not get translated to moral actions and upright living that impacts the world but is relegated to the private realm. Worse yet, knowledge without an ethical burden can mutate into a means to gain power over others. Groome explains: "'Forgetfulness of being' and 'triumph of mind' combine to encourage education that perpetuates unjust social arrangements, precisely because it excludes significant aspects of human 'being' and the majority of human beings from the 'knowledge' that wields social power; it maintains an epistemic privilege of a few over the rest."[10]

Theology's rehabilitation of wisdom reestablishes ethics in the epistemological domain and with it the recognition that theology has a practical pastoral function, "assisting people to enjoy and glorify God."[11] Ethics and theology are thus intricately connected: theology's pastoral function cannot be fulfilled without Christian ethical commitment to human flourishing and active participation in the public discourse on human rights, power, and justice from a biblical understanding of equality and justice. Theology is not an ideological speech about God that has no bearing on everyday matters of living and dying in the world. Rather, it is a public act, and the community of faith is the public church. A renewed commitment to Christian ethics means breaking down the walls that have confined theology to the private realm or to the academic ivory tower and unleashing it to the public where it belongs.

Interconnectivity of Knowledge

Postmodernism also demonstrates a movement from *epistemological foundationalism* to *holism*. With the widespread recognition that even scientific facts are theory laden, the cornerstone of empiricist foundationalism

10. Groome, *Sharing Faith*, 8.
11. Vanhoozer, *Drama of Doctrine*, 13.

representing the modern paradigm began to crumble. The philosophical world became more acutely aware that "what is indubitable in one intellectual context is all too questionable in another."[12] With the infallibility of knowledge challenged, an alternative way of understanding the world emerged known as *holism*. In this view, knowledge is seen not as a firm foundation but as a complex web or a system of beliefs that provides mutual and interactive support. No one component of that system is sufficient for characterizing the properties of the whole, but each part is dependent on others, and they must all be considered together. In contrast to foundationalism, which treats knowledge or truth as being "out there" and open to isolated and individual discoveries, holism calls attention to the *interconnectivity of knowledge*. The concept of holism takes a prominent place in our postmodern consciousness, which emphasizes the community's role in holding together multitudes of smaller fragments of truths. "Beliefs are held to be true within the context of [the] communities that espouse them,"[13] and it is in this sense that "postmodern truth is [considered] relative to the community in which a person participates."[14] Truth is largely articulated and formulated by the operative rules and dynamics of the community instead of waiting to be discovered and verified by its own objective "truthfulness."

Thomas Kuhn's influential work *The Structure of Scientific Revolutions* has received simultaneously the highest acclaim and the sharpest of criticisms. One reason for this mixed review is the challenge it presents to the rationality of natural science and how it spotlights the communal practice of science. Overturning the normative view of scientific developments as steady, cumulative progress toward pure facts or objective truths, Kuhn instead describes scientific development as being noncumulative developmental episodes.[15] The scientific community handles received beliefs and defends those assumptions by "forc[ing] nature into the conceptual boxes" of preexisting categories of knowledge in periods of normal science. The field of science undergoes a paradigm shift when anomalies occur that

---

12. Nancey Murphy, *Beyond Liberalism and Fundamentalism: How Modern and Postmodern Philosophy Set the Theological Agenda* (Harrisburg, PA: Trinity Press, 1996), 91.

13. Stanley J. Grenz, *A Primer on Postmodernism* (Grand Rapids: Eerdmans, 1996), 15.

14. Grenz, *Primer on Postmodernism*, 14.

15. Thomas S. Kuhn, *The Structure of Scientific Revolutions*, 3rd ed. (Chicago: University of Chicago Press, 1996), 92.

"subvert the existing tradition of scientific practice"[16] and require us to reassess accepted assumptions and formulate new stances. When existing rules of science fail to adequately solve a problem, the community responds to the crisis by raising competing proposals, each candidate attempting to explain the situation more aptly than its rivals have. The winner of the "paradigm wars" is essentially determined by who garners the greatest amount of support from the scientific community. Scientists "convert" to a particular paradigm for many reasons (e.g., the paradigm's ability to solve problems better than competitors; personal and subjective preference for how "neat," "suitable," or "simple" it is;[17] promise for future research), but ultimately "what occurs is an increasing shift in the distribution of professional allegiances."[18] Eventually many in the community will accept the new paradigm as normative and readjust to the new set of basic assumptions brought on by the "scientific revolution."

Admittedly, this brief summary does not do justice to the complexity and ramifications of Kuhn's most-known writing. The summary serves only to highlight his argument for the "incommensurability" of scientific theories (i.e., there is no common measure by which to consider theories) and the critical role that the community plays in selecting theories that will determine the present norms and the future direction of science.[19] Kuhn's work questions the positivistic view of reality and attempts to show that what is long accepted as normative—even in science—is much more a product of communal interpretation and intersubjectivity than was previously thought.

Perception of Language as a Social Phenomenon That Shapes Reality

Another postmodern shift is *the perception of language as a social phenomenon (i.e., created through social interactions) that shapes reality.* Modernity held out a representational theory of perception and a correspondence theory of truth that construed language as a "mirror of nature"

16. Kuhn, *Structure of Scientific Revolutions*, 5, 6.
17. Kuhn, *Structure of Scientific Revolutions*, 150.
18. Kuhn, *Structure of Scientific Revolutions*, 158.
19. Since the original publication of *The Structure of Scientific Revolutions* in 1962, Kuhn's ideas concerning scientific incommensurability underwent several modifications that adapted to the criticisms he received.

reflecting reality as it actually is.[20] An unbreakable and unmistakable bond was thought to exist between language and the truth to which it points. This link, once thought to conjoin language and reality, was severed with the postmodern assault on epistemological foundationalism. As a result, "language once adequately expressed a particular relationship to reality, but now when we, whose relationship to reality has changed, use the same words, they become untrue. They cease to be a means of grasping and comprehending reality."[21]

Rather than a static entity that renders one preexisting meaning in reference to the external world, language is now understood as a socially constructed, self-referential system by which the differences among words relay meaning.[22] Conversely, language is also believed to have the power to shape reality. Words not only represent ideas, feelings, and the state of things but are also performative utterances that shape new realities (e.g., the command "Go!" produces an action of departure).[23] With the power to create reality ascribed to language, "the ultimate certainty of the Cartesian 'I think' is taken over by the certainty of 'I speak.' The reality of language becomes the ground of certainty. Consciousness thus gives way to language. Before, consciousness was regarded as the ground and presupposition of language. But now, it is language which gives consciousness its form and content. And the logic of language becomes the controlling center."[24]

If the modernist understanding of the function of words is represented by the metaphor of language as a mirror, then the postmodernist image is "language as a tool or language as action"[25] that constructs social reality.

From the postmodern perspective, language is not a neutral instrument but is historically and socially conditioned. Language is seen as an unreliable tool used by those who possess social and political power to shape and

20. Richard Rorty, *Philosophy and the Mirror of Nature* (Princeton: Princeton University Press, 1979).

21. Helmut Thielicke, *The Trouble with the Church*, trans. John W. Doberstein (New York: Harper & Row, 1965), 45.

22. See Ferdinand de Saussure, *Course in General Linguistics*, trans. Wade Baskin (New York: Columbia University Press, 1959).

23. J. L. Austin, *How to Do Things with Words* (Oxford: Oxford University Press, 1962).

24. Carver Yu, "Truth and Authentic Humanity," plenary address at the Gospel and Our Culture National Swanwick Consultation, Swanwick, UK, July 1992. See www.gospel-culture .org.uk.

25. Murphy, *Beyond Liberalism and Fundamentalism*, 111.

control the culture. Jacques Derrida points out an embedded hierarchy in the metaphysics of language itself.[26] The way he sees it, language is structured as binary oppositions (e.g., presence/absence; writing/speech; mind/body; perception/reason) in which one side of the dichotomy is privileged while the other is marginalized. While there may be various reasons for this imbalance, the preference for one over its counterpart stems largely from how human perceptions work to make one thing seem more normative, true, or valuable than another. Be that as it may, Derrida argues that the poison of linguistic prejudice must be neutralized through deconstructionism, which uncovers the long-existing social blind spots and names what has been excluded and marginalized in the process.[27] By exposing the partiality of language, Derrida goes against the Western world's logocentricism (i.e., the assumption that language mediates the presence of an external reality and thus carries an intrinsic meaning) and reveals that the normative values in the culture are actually products of social construction.

If the quintessential feature of cultural postmodernism is "incredulity toward metanarratives,"[28] suspicion toward language and its use is another expression of that disbelief. Carver Yu aptly describes the prevailing mood of today's culture as one of "technological optimism and literary despair."[29] Disillusioned by the ideology and limitations of language, suspicion stemming from despair is the postmodern mode of approaching texts.

Turn to Communal Authority

Another key shift resulting from modern to postmodern epistemology is *the translocation of authority from an individual knower to a community of people.* Modernity sought to "purify the operations of human reason by decontextualizing them: i.e., by divorcing them from the details of particular historical and cultural situations"[30] in order to isolate ubiquitous rules and logic that govern nature and rationality. Science and reason

26. Jacques Derrida, *Of Grammatology* (Baltimore: Johns Hopkins University Press, 1976).
27. See Jacques Derrida, *Dissemination* (Chicago: University of Chicago Press, 1983).
28. Jean-François Lyotard, *The Postmodern Condition: A Report on Knowledge* (Minneapolis: University of Minnesota Press, 1984), xxiv.
29. Yu, "Truth and Authentic Humanity."
30. Stephen Toulmin, *Cosmopolis: The Hidden Agenda of Modernity* (Chicago: University of Chicago Press, 1990), 104.

were regarded as definitive pathways to timeless, universal truths of divine revelation embedded and accessible in creation—and the autonomous, thinking human was the arbiter of those truths. This view led to disclaiming four kinds of practical knowledge in place of another kind:

- rejection of the oral for the written (preference for proofs and formal logic over rhetoric);
- rejection of the particular for the universal (preference for general principles over specific cases);
- rejection of the local for the general (preference for abstract axioms over concrete diversity); and
- rejection of the timely for the timeless (preference for permanence over the transitory).[31]

Yet the tides are changing again in this era. The transitions under way in the present epistemological realm are a direct reversal of what modernism constructed: *a rejection of the written for the oral, the universal for the particular, the general for the local, and the timeless for the timely.*[32]

Dethroning the notion of a self-evident, overarching, and supracultural fixed truth, postmoderns cleave to transient truth that bends and molds to take the eclectic shapes of sundry cultures, contexts, and perspectives. Descartes's independent, conscious self is no longer the reality-defining measure; truth and knowledge are considered social constructs that occur because of and for communities. We see that totalizing, authoritarian knowledge claims often meet resistance in today's culture, as metanarratives are "considered modernist ploys to legitimize the power of those in authority; they are nothing more than propaganda meant to impose particular preferences on others."[33] In an "antiauthority" culture,

> minds cannot be organized and thoughts cannot be forced on people. No institution, however venerable, has the right to impose an idea upon us by the weight of its own authority. Nor even can any idea impose itself upon us all. For there is no such thing as a truth which is absolute and therefore

---

31. Toulmin, *Cosmopolis*, 30–35.
32. Toulmin, *Cosmopolis*, 186–89.
33. Anderson, *Shape of Practical Theology*, 19.

universal. On the contrary, everything is relative and subjective. Before I can believe any idea, it has to authenticate itself to me personally; and before you can be expected to believe it, it must become self-authenticating to you. Until this happens, we neither should nor can believe.[34]

Everyone is an authority in their own right: they talk about reality as they see it from their own social location. The pursuit of knowledge is not a privilege of some but the basic right and expression of life for all those who think, feel, and experience the world. No one interpretation is definitive; all interpretation is tentative and always subject to revision in the give-and-take with others. The collection of ideas and perspectives constituting a community is the new epistemological authority in this postmodern era.

The Postmodern Ethos and the Conversational Homiletic

The six major shifts discussed above underscore the basic assumptions and values of the conversational homiletic that was birthed from the womb of postmodernism. Resisting the noxious dichotomy of theory and practice, the conversationalists insist that Scripture should be read and preached in light of the church's ongoing experience in the world. Practice should inform theology and preaching, and conversely, theology and preaching should inform practical living. In this way not only is the starting point for theology and preaching redefined (i.e., not theoretical inquiry but lived experience of people) but so also are their parameters and final goal (i.e., to inform everyday behaviors). Preaching is thus a creative exploration of what it means for believers to be physical, social, historical, and cultural beings in light of their faith in Jesus Christ.

The clarion call of the conversationalists is that the church must move past an individualistic faith and private ethic and lean into the *telos* of demonstrating love for God and neighbors through good works in the public realm, like "a city set on a hill" (Matt. 5:14). Although the church's final goal and terminus is the world beyond our walls, where systemic issues of power and injustice must be confronted in Jesus's name, the first

---

34. John Stott, *Between Two Worlds: The Challenge of Preaching Today* (Grand Rapids: Eerdmans, 1982), 55–56.

stop on this journey is the pulpit, where the inequality in the relationship between the minister and the congregation beckons to be revised. Conversationalists assert that if the church is to be known as a countercultural community marked by justice and compassion in the world, the pulpit needs to be the first place to model hospitable love that welcomes all and gives ear to every voice. To this end, they remind us that the priesthood of all believers becomes a lived reality only when the congregation is treated as agent-subjects who share the responsibilities to interpret Scripture and contribute to the proclamations that nourish the community's spiritual formation. Conversational scholars deny the attainability of a self-evident, value-free truth and consider reality a product of linguistic construction through human interactions. In this light, revealed knowledge and the single authority of a preacher no longer constitute the indubitable basis of epistemic justification; knowledge is believed to be a community's network of perspectives, stories, and experiences in which all members share the power to shape narratives, identity, and reality.

Strengths of the Conversational Homiletic

The conversational model holds promise in areas where the traditional model has been found lacking. Since the previous chapter noted many strengths of the conversational homiletic, only a few additional ones are listed here. First, an obvious strength of the conversational model is its taking seriously the large-scale metamorphosis from modernism to postmodernism and proactively responding to the adaptive challenges brought on by epistemological and cultural shifts with a fresh vision for preaching. Rather than shying away and hoping for simpler days to return, conversational preachers embrace the uncertainty, disorientation, and messiness of this era, along with its potential, and invite other preachers to join them in being the wineskin prepared to receive the new wine of the Spirit's work in today's world. They offer an important, timely reminder: the church must "respond to the present and participate in the shaping of the future."[35]

35. O. Wesley Allen Jr., *The Homiletic of All Believers: A Conversational Approach* (Louisville: Westminster John Knox, 2005), 5.

Second, the conversationalists remind us that hermeneutics is an on-going process and an open-ended communication built on the values of respect, patience, and hospitality for others. It follows that the role of biblical hermeneutics is to foster cordial and genuine dialogue on the meaning and significance of Scripture in church amid the complexities of the human pre-understanding, condition, and relationships, which play into interpretation. If openness and receptivity to others' ideas, humility in our own beliefs, and curiosity and readiness for new learning and experiences no longer characterize our hermeneutical work, and if we are instead more fixated on the finality of meaning and in reaching a consensus of interpretation, we may be missing the point of biblical hermeneutics. The conversational model renews the proper role of hermeneutics in preaching by rectifying modernity's view of texts as univocal and inert and interpretation as restrictive and closed.

Third, the conversational proponents caution against reducing God's vast and infinite Word into an atomity of human understanding, particularly into manageable forms of propositional one-liners and gospel nuggets. A faithful reading of Scripture as God's Word requires that we remain open to new, surprising things about God and his ability to communicate that simultaneously strengthen our faith and shatter our formerly held convictions, expanding the horizons of our understanding. For preachers, the willingness to reappraise our views and convictions means in part "a turn to listeners" and being more intimately acquainted with the congregation's stories and their on-the-ground reflections on what God through the Scriptures is saying and doing today. Congregational stories are not mere embellishments to sermons or rhetorical tactics used to connect with hearers and earn their trust. The collective wisdom, gifts, thoughts, and experiences represented in a congregation provide one window into God's missional activities today and the continuing fulfillment of his promises.

Lastly, the conversational model celebrates the mysteries and tensions in faith and restores poetic and metaphoric language to the pulpit. The conversational proponents assert that language has no direct, unalterable correspondence to one ultimate reality, and thus preaching language, too, is an approximation of the divine. Even the most eloquent sermon is a feeble attempt at evoking the transcendent: "All that we can do is . . . to 'set right one error of expression by another,' seeking thereby to 'steady our minds, not so as to reach their object, but to point them in the right direction.'"[36] This kind of preaching does not provide a set answer to resolve every apprehension in life but instead equips the church to live in the awkward tension of being salt and light in a decaying, dark world. The language that best fits this peculiar task is metaphoric and poetic. In contrast to discursive language, which prioritizes precision, clarity, and reasonableness, the language of evocation values ambiguity and openness and makes no certain promises on what the deep journey into the text means for readers. It frees people "to put aside the objectifying pose and to experience reality in personal and suggestive ways"[37] so that they are empowered from the inside out to stand in tension-filled places in the world as a physical symbol of God's steadfast presence.

Preliminary Concerns and Questions

Although the conversational model is promising in many regards, it raises several concerns and questions that deserve attention.[38] Take the role of preaching in the conversational model. The conversationalists claim that preaching serves to foster dialogue and refocus the church's central conversations around Scripture. Yet if this is all preaching is, how is it distinct from other conversations in the church? If the pulpit's principal function is to stimulate godly conversations or "God-talks" (however that is defined) that reverberate from the ecclesial community to the world, why not bypass the pulpit to adopt more sensible and effective strategies to achieve this goal (e.g., intimate settings of small groups, Bible study, one-on-one mentorship)? Also, if the sermon is merely a tentative interpretation, wager, or proposal (as Rose says) or a report on the conversational dynamics of a pre-sermon group (as McClure asserts) or vocabulary lessons that supply

36. Nicholas Lash quotes John Henry Newman from *The Theological Papers of John Henry Newman on Faith and Certainty*, ed. J. Derek Holmes (Oxford: Clarendon, 1976), 102. See Nicholas Lash, *Holiness, Speech, and Silence: Reflections on the Question of God* (Burlington, VT: Ashgate, 2004), 51–52.

37. Don Wardlaw, "Introduction: The Need for New Shapes," in *Preaching Biblically*, ed. Don Wardlaw (Philadelphia: Westminster John Knox, 1983), 19.

38. A disclaimer ought to be given that, since the works of Rose, McClure, and Allen represent three distinct approaches to conversational preaching, some weaknesses discussed in this section might be more applicable to the ideas of one scholar over others.

the congregation with religious language in their meaning-making (as Allen suggests), then in what way is *Christian* preaching unique? How is the proclamation of the gospel different from other competing religious, political, or cultural discourses that also strive to make a difference in people's lives and the world at large?

This bleeds into another concern and question, which has to do with the role of ministers in the conversational model. Rose argues, "The most fundamental problem with traditional preaching is that it is predicated on a gap that separates the preacher and the congregation. Rather, for [advocates of conversational preaching] the primary relationship is solidarity and mutuality. Our image of preaching does not presuppose a sense of separation between the preacher as a sender and the congregation as recipients [of communication]. Instead, more fundamental than differences between the preacher and the congregation are experiences of belonging, shared identity, and mutual interdependency."[39]

Her words hint at an odd polarity of two mutually exclusive options that face the preacher: *separation* from the congregation predicated by one's belief in ministerial authority or *solidarity* with the congregation by choosing communal equality. Yet is this indeed the case? Is it fair to say that the abdication of ministerial authority is the only way to ensure unity between the preacher and the congregation? Furthermore, if ministers should be fundamentally indistinguishable from other members of the congregation except in their theological training and ministry experience, what real need is there, if any, for ordained clergy? Why, then, does the Bible painstakingly highlight the election, calling, and equipping of those who are called to be the overseers of the church (Eph. 4:11; Col. 1:25; 1 Thess. 2:4; 1 Tim. 2:7)? Why does Scripture repeatedly portray the Holy Spirit's diverse spiritual gifting for the edification of the church (Rom. 12:3–8; 1 Cor. 12:4–11; Eph. 4:11–16; 1 Pet. 4:10–11)? The conversationalists desire the equality of all believers. Even so, stripping the pulpit of its authority does not guarantee an equal hearing and respect for every voice. The Spirit who calls the church to mutual edification has supplied manifold gifts within the body to do so, and the priesthood of

39. Lucy Atkinson Rose, *Sharing the Word: Preaching in the Roundtable Church* (Louisville: Westminster John Knox, 1997), 21–22.

all believers is not synonymous with homogeneity of roles and functions of equally valuable body parts.

Another concern relates to the precarious claim made by the conversationalists that knowledge (i.e., truth) is pieced together by sundry perspectives and viewpoints. If meaning is a joint construction and the church's confidence to understand God rests on a social practice of those who read the Bible, it raises a practical missiological question: What implication does this have for numerous Christians around the world whose freedom to gather with other believers is limited at best? Is the Bible any less truthful or meaningful for those who lack the interpretive quorum? It is worth pondering whether every interpretation should be weighed with an equal sense of validity in a setting where most are nonbelievers and new converts to faith. If the majority of those who are present come to learn and be "indoctrinated" into Christian faith—that is, to be imbued with the faith-cultivating instructions of the Bible and the Christian tradition—what might a constructive dialogue look like in that setting? Also, how can pastors with limited or no Christian resources learn and become equipped with the emotional, communicational, and relational skills to listen actively and to competently facilitate deep, honest discussions, and even navigate complex group dynamics? Finally, is there really a place for rebuke, confrontation, and excommunication in the conversational model? How does the church determine what is heretical and a perversion of the gospel if the ecclesial community possesses greater authority than the Scripture's own internal witness does?

Two Underlying Problems of the Conversational Model

At the heart of the concerns and questions raised in the preceding section lies the issue of biblical hermeneutics: how the church interprets the Bible and lives according to its claims. Numerous angles from which to examine this issue exist, but to limit the scope of the discussion, we will focus on two central hermeneutical problems in the conversational model: (1) the loss of confidence in Scripture's ability to communicate a discernible meaning, and (2) the turn to the community of readers to generate meaning as a solution to this perceived problem.

The Loss of Confidence in the Bible to Convey Meaning

Since words and the reality they signify have no intrinsic relationship, and meaning is a product of social construction, the culture exhibits a growing sense of disillusionment toward language. There is a widespread recognition that human beings are nonneutral interpreters who are historically located and partial to their own interests and to the interests of their community. Such views of people and the way the world operates go beyond impacting the secular culture and profoundly inform the church's reading of Scripture. Since the rise of Protestantism, the Bible has long been regarded as the church's primary source for faith and practice. Even through hardships, the reforming church fought to abide by its confession of *sola Scriptura*. In recent times, the meaning of the formal principle of the Reformation has come under scrutiny as people began raising questions about whose interpretation the church is referring to when it speaks of "the Word of God." Whose thoughts and experiences are being reflected when the church speaks of truth? Which groups are being excluded in the process? Influenced by the "masters of suspicion,"[40] much of postmodern biblical interpretation has become linked with investigating and exposing the political dynamics of power that are believed to govern all texts, as well as the world at large.

The same disillusionment can be detected in the conversational model. Language has come to be regarded as an unreliable medium that is manipulated to legitimize and regulate the ideological pursuits that benefit some and that result in the oppression of many. This is true of all language, including religious language. Rose claims that "all language, including the language of faith, is inevitably biased and limited, historically conditioned, and inseparable from the sins of each generation and each community of users."[41] For this reason, religious language (including the language of the Bible and the words from the pulpit) can function as a tool for hegemony, bigotry, and injustice (e.g., legitimizing slavery or the unequal treatment of women). Rose goes so far as to argue that the common deficiency of popular preaching models is that "they do not discuss *the problem of the fallen nature of language* in general."[42]

---

40. Paul Ricoeur, *Freud and Philosophy: An Essay on Interpretation* (New Haven: Yale University Press, 1970), 32.

41. Rose, *Sharing the Word*, 90.

42. Rose, *Sharing the Word*, 81 (emphasis added).

Since all language is "fallen," the conversational preachers approach the Bible with a sense of skepticism and caution. The language of the Bible also cannot escape the postmodern impasse in which meaning eludes the author and the reader. The interpretation of Scripture, then, "giv[es] way . . . to deconstructive dissemination"[43] in which "the boundaries between the [biblical] writer and reader disappear, replaced by this womb of textuality in which writer and reader weave together 'yet more shimmering webs of undecidability stretching to the horizon.'"[44] Denying the attainability of meaning, the conversationalists assert, "The grand narratives of a unified biblical text and a unitary gospel to preach are fast disappearing."[45]

> In light of this view of language, what preachers must do is [exit] from a unitary exegetical method [and embrace] a deconstructive *resistance to the traditional idea of a unitary transcendent and masterful (A)author behind every author of the biblical text.* The final origin or authority behind the text is a disseminated authority, an author who is neither beyond nor in the text, but somewhere between the lines. *This author is . . . a complex multiplicity of interwoven voices striving to be born from a womb of words that constantly defers presence.*[46]

To the conversational scholars, it is this deferral—the constant seeking of meaning and the searching for the presence of the *otherness* of the text—that precisely defines the Scripture and the ministry of preaching. Although there are "momentary arrestings of the flow of connotations and interpretive possibilities"[47] that lend to the occasion of preaching and liturgy, even those moments are not permanent and are meant only to encourage the community toward a continual exploration of meaning. Scripture practices deconstructive erasure of all positions and identities so that readers are constantly moving in proximity to *others*.[48] To those

---

43. John S. McClure, *Other-Wise Preaching: A Postmodern Ethic for Homiletics* (St. Louis: Chalice, 2001), 14.
44. McClure quotes from Terry Eagleton, *Literary Theory: An Introduction* (Oxford: Oxford University Press, 1983), 146. See McClure, *Other-Wise Preaching*, 17.
45. McClure, *Other-Wise Preaching*, 13.
46. McClure, *Other-Wise Preaching*, 14 (emphasis added).
47. McClure, *Other-Wise Preaching*, 21–22.
48. McClure defines "other-wise homiletics" as preaching that "because of its orientation toward the stranger, becomes patently other-wise than homiletics itself, that is, it seeks to place the

who object that the centripetal quality of the Bible that erases all positions appears to "be no position at all or, perhaps every position at the same time," McClure responds: "This . . . is precisely the case."[49] Rather than being concerned with the meaning of the text, the nature of Scripture and, consequently, preaching is to exercise deconstructive erasure so that it continues to point readers to people around them.

A Critical Realistic Stance

The hermeneutical stance of the conversationalists nevertheless poses an important question: Could a text that is always under deconstructive erasure and therefore has no clear position offer something worthy ("meaningful") to preach? Deconstruction has a necessary place in the reading of Scripture—namely, it unmasks the idols that we hold as absolutes.[50] Nonetheless, the danger of deconstructionism as the only or even the governing mode of hermeneutics is that nothing would be left for the church to believe and profess in the end. When the church loses confidence in Scripture and its ability to convey a distinct, understandable message, the significance and urgency of preaching also disappear. Ronald Allen agrees: "Deconstruction only exposes and eliminates. When serving as a community's only interpretive activity, deconstruction leaves a community without a symbolic universe because every symbol has been deconstructed. The center of the community's life is void. . . . Consequently, a community is left in uncertainty and perhaps chaos."[51]

The prophetic ministry of preaching must expose and name our sins of partiality and bigotry and the ugly reality of suffering and evil in the world. It remains an imperious task for preachers to urge people to humbly and bravely face what is happening around the world by assessing where they are and what part they play in this broken ecosystem. Whatever else preaching may be, it is surely more than calling attention to the social powers that influence human understanding of language, one another, and the world.

---

totality of homiletics under deconstructive erasure so that preaching might be transformed by a profound awareness of the proximity to preaching's 'others.'" McClure, *Other-Wise Preaching*, xi.

49. McClure, *Other-Wise Preaching*, 21.

50. Ronald J. Allen, *Preaching and the Other: Studies of Postmodern Insights* (St. Louis: Chalice, 2009), 69–70.

51. R. Allen, *Preaching and the Other*, 70.

Sermons do more than tell people what the Bible stands *against*; they also point people to what the Bible is *for*—or more precisely, they orient people to the reality that God is *for* us. Conversationalists' perspectives may be animated by a sincere desire to confront the pulpit's partiality to one particular way of reading and preaching from the Bible. But by denying the existence and the attainability of a determinate meaning of Scripture, conversational preachers inadvertently strip Scripture of meaning as the unique, authoritative Word of God that is truly *other* than us. Warning against a skeptical approach to reading the Bible with the driving interest to dismantle its internal structure, Allen cautions that deconstructionism "must be accompanied by construction." He writes, "A community needs to construct a symbolic universe that helps it understand the nature and purpose of the various elements of life and how they relate with one another in optimum ways. . . . On the one hand, the preacher needs to *help the congregation identify a Christian worldview* in which the congregation can have *confidence*. On the other hand, the preacher must recognize that aspects of a Christian worldview *can* (and sometimes should) be deconstructed."[52]

Allen's words resonate with the critical realistic stance that this book subscribes to.[53] Critical realism holds that the church's interpretation of Scripture should exist in the tension of "both maintaining that theories describe things that exist (hence, 'realism') and that theories can be true or false (hence, 'critical')."[54] Thus preachers who hold this position do not speak with certainty or bullheaded insistence on the claims they make. That being said, the awareness of their epistemological limitation as situated knowers does not hamper their reasonable assurance in an external reality to which they can point and have meaningful conversations. To a critical realist, "authorial intentionality as an external reality must be the controlling factor for interpretation."[55] Hence there is a balance of provi-

---

52. R. Allen, *Preaching and the Other*, 70 (emphasis added).

53. See Ben Meyer, *Critical Realism and the New Testament* (Allison Park, PA: Pickwick, 1989); Meyer, *Reality and Illusion in New Testament Scholarship: A Primer in Critical Realist Hermeneutics* (Collegeville, MN: Liturgical Press, 1994); N. T. Wright, *Christian Origins and the Question of God*, vol. 1, *The New Testament and the People of God* (Minneapolis: Fortress, 1992).

54. Kevin Vanhoozer, *Is There a Meaning in This Text? The Bible, the Reader, and the Morality of Literary Knowledge* (Grand Rapids: Zondervan, 1998), 322.

55. Thorsten Moritz, "Critical Realism," in *Dictionary for Theological Interpretation of the Bible*, ed. Kevin J. Vanhoozer (Grand Rapids: Baker Academic, 2005), 149.

sionality and openness to change on one hand and, on the other, trust and confidence that Scripture has both discernible meaning and propositional content that can ground preaching.

Rethinking Language and Authority

In contrast to postmodernism's suspicious take on language and authority, this book advocates the counterbalance of an auspicious view of language and authority that reframes the conversationalists' understanding.[56] The concern of the conversational preachers regarding language and its use in the pulpit warrants the church's deep reflection, which will hopefully lead to genuine change. The conversationalists' words ring painfully true when we assess the state of preaching today. Many pulpits not only suffer from the same linguistic prejudice of the culture but also show partiality to the language of certitude at the expense of evocative language, which leaves the church spiritually, emotionally, and imaginatively undernourished. Eugene Peterson agrees: "Too often the living Word is desiccated into propositional cadavers, then sorted into exegetical specimens in bottles of formaldehyde."[57] Such preaching results in "the separation of method of preaching from theology of preaching [which] is a violation, leaving not one but two orphans."[58]

Notwithstanding these kinds of issues, we need to be cautious about quickly sharing in the conversationalists' disillusionment toward language, for this can easily lead to literary despair. It is one thing to be perturbed about the nonneutrality of language and quite another to dispose of all trust in language. It is one thing to be unsettled by how language can be mishandled and exploited to gain ascendancy over others; it is something else altogether to permit this recognition to take on a life of its own and dictate how we as the church see the Bible.

In contrast to the postmodern despair over language, a Christian attitude toward language must be infused with comfort and hope in God's

56. See later in this chapter for further discussion regarding the need for the hermeneutic of suspicion (i.e., a deconstructive approach that challenges the world of hegemonic powers) and the need to balance it with the hermeneutic of trust (i.e., a constructive approach that points a way forward for a possible world of meaning and significance) when reading texts.

57. Eugene Peterson, *Tell It Slant: A Conversation on the Language of Jesus in His Stories and Prayers* (Grand Rapids: Eerdmans, 2008), 1.

58. Fred B. Craddock, *As One without Authority*, 4th ed. (St. Louis: Chalice, 2001), 43.

creational goodness and redemption through Christ. This stance is exemplified by Eugene Peterson, who is burdened along with the conversationalists by language and its use, but he does not remain despondent. Peterson admits that language, indeed, can function as an instrument of oppression. He is also aware that the language of preaching often does not "savor subtleties" or "relish ambiguities"[59] but more zealously establishes absolutes. Even so, he suggests that we do not have to fall prey to the malady of postmodern cynicism toward language: "Language, all of it—every vowel, every consonant—is a gift of God. God uses language to create and command us; we use language to confess our sins and sing praises to God. We use this very same language getting to know one another. . . . We use the same words in talking to one another that we use when we're talking to God: same nouns and verbs, same prepositions and pronouns."[60]

One can detect affinity in Kevin Vanhoozer's writing as he suggests how to properly combat the postmodern distrust of language: "We must therefore counter the postmodern despair of language with Christian *delight*, and the main reason we can delight in language is that we believe language is God-given (and hence reliable), and that we believe there is something beyond language to which our poems, our propositions and our prayers all point: the reality of the Creator and the created order."[61]

A Christian understanding of language—even including the limitations and problems of its "fall"—needs to be framed by the biblical story of God, who out of his goodness and benevolence created the world and is renewing it through Christ. We must "refuse to let Babel [i.e., the symbol of breakdown in human communication resulting from sin] be the first and last word, and . . . insist on contextualizing Babel within creation, fall and redemption."[62] The remembrance of God's grand narrative overcomes the postmodern fixation on Babel and balances with Pentecost, which "signifies the reverse of Babel, to be consummated in the new heavens and new earth in which linguistic pluralism celebrates Messiah."[63]

---

59. Peterson, *Tell It Slant*, 3.
60. Peterson, *Tell It Slant*, 2.
61. Kevin Vanhoozer, *First Theology: God, Scripture, and Hermeneutics* (Downers Grove, IL: InterVarsity Press, 2002), 33.
62. Craig G. Bartholomew, "Babel and Derrida: Postmodernism, Language, and Biblical Interpretation," *Tyndale Bulletin* 49, no. 2 (1998): 327.
63. Bartholomew, "Babel and Derrida," 327–28.

Likewise, the concept of authority that generates palpable antagonism in the postmodern culture needs reframing. Authority need not be perceived as something that stands against people, holding the whip-hand in dominating others and restraining their potential. On the contrary, authority from a Christian perspective is an enabling, emancipatory power issued by God for the flourishing of others. This can be glimpsed in the first pages of the Bible when humankind is given dominion over creation (Gen. 1:26) and told to subdue the earth (1:28). Not in the least is this text an endorsement for mistreating and abusing creation. The Creator bestows humankind with the power to rule and govern. This empowers us as responsible servants and stewards who, in the likeness of God, care and show kindness to creation so that it can thrive and prosper. N. T. Wright applies this understanding of authority to Scripture:

> Authority is not the power to control people, and crush them, and keep them in little boxes. . . . Nor is the Bible as the vehicle of God's authority meant to be information for the legalist. . . . Rather, God's authority vested in scripture is designated, as all God's authority is designed, to liberate human beings, to judge and condemn evil and sin in the world in order to set people free to be fully human. . . . That is what his authority is there *for*. And when we use a shorthand phrase like "authority of scripture" that is what we ought to be meaning. It is an authority with this shape and character, this purpose and goal.[64]

If this is the nature of the Bible's authority, the problems arise not when making authoritative claims in preaching but when preachers attempt to "remove those claims from scrutiny, critique, and even refutation."[65]

The Turn to the Community to Generate Meaning

The conversational model has a second hermeneutical problem. When people lose confidence in Scripture to convey a clear, discernible message, it falls to the community of readers to generate meaning from their experience of the text. We see that the foundationalism of the traditional

64. N. T. Wright, "How Can the Bible Be Authoritative?," *Vox Evangelica* 21 (1991): 16.
65. Lose, *Confessing Jesus Christ*, 163.

homiletic has been replaced by the relational epistemology of the conversational homiletic. Thus the once culturally acceptable statement "We hold these truths to be self-evident" has been replaced with "Our socially constructed selves arbitrarily agree that certain chunks of language are to be esteemed in our linguistic community."[66] Grant Osborne explains this postmodern phenomenon:

> The [post]modern critics increasingly deny the very possibility of discovering the original, or intended, meaning of a text. The problem is that while the original authors had a definite meaning in mind when they wrote, that is now lost to us because they are no longer present to clarify and explain what they wrote. The [post]modern reader cannot study the text from the ancient perspective but constantly reads into that passage [post]modern perspectives. . . . Every community provides traditions to guide the reader in comprehending a text, and these produce the meaning. That "meaning" differs from community to community, so in actuality any passage might have multiple meanings, and each is valid for a particular reading perspective or community.[67]

Since the authorial intent of Scripture is deemed inaccessible, the conversational proponents claim that "the meaning and truth of words . . . lie more in their *use* than in their reference."[68] The conversational homiletic is therefore a consensus-based epistemological model that stresses the *value* of texts rather than their *historicity*, *facticity*, or *truthfulness*. With pragmatism and functionality as the new basis from which to evaluate orthodoxy, the criterion for interpretation is "whether sermonic interpretations, proposals, and wagers serve to foster all the central conversations of the church as the people of God, whether they upbuild the communities of faith in their local and global configurations, and whether they respect and invite the voices of the silenced, the disenfranchised, the poor, and women."[69]

66. J. P. Moreland, "Truth, Contemporary Philosophy, and the Postmodern Turn" (presentation, Evangelical Theological Society, San Antonio, TX, November 18, 2004).
67. Grant R. Osborne, *The Hermeneutical Spiral: A Comprehensive Introduction to Biblical Interpretation* (Downers Grove, IL: InterVarsity Press, 1991), 7.
68. McClure, *Other-Wise Preaching*, 100.
69. Rose, *Sharing the Word*, 106.

The conversational preachers assure us that their interpretive imagination stays within the parameters of communal testimony (i.e., what the Bible means to others) in order to steer clear of relativism. As far as Rose is concerned, a more pertinent question of biblical hermeneutics asks, "Who exercises control over the interpretive process and therefore over preaching's content?" This question is important to Rose because it exposes that "those who exercise control over preaching's content are, in fact, all those who are invited to participate in the formative conversations of the people of God," and if "every interpretation of every text is freighted with the biases of the interpreters, then the text alone is not an adequate safeguard."[70] What is the ultimate safeguard then? Mistrusting the biblical text's authority and agenda, the conversational preachers make their own decisive claim regarding where interpretive authority lies when the church reads the Bible: the intersubjectivity of readers.

However, elevating the interpretive community's authority over Scripture's authority brings clear dangers. First, divine authorial intent is stripped from texts as the Bible is treated like a blank canvas on which readers can project whatever they fancy. In doing so, meaning is subject to the whims of those engaged in interpretation. Conversational preachers say that the turn to others is an act of social justice extended for equality and liberation of all people, but disregarding the text's own voice is an act of "interpretive violence,"[71] and ironic injustice is committed against the divine author and Scripture's human writers.

Second, giving precedence to human subjectivism is both absurd and inimical to fruitful hermeneutics. At one level, it is strange and senseless that "experience (of a certain sort) is treated as unambiguously revelatory, and the Bible is critically scrutinized in its light."[72] At another level, such an approach to texts is counterproductive, considering how the variety and diversity of human experiences can have any jurisdiction over what constitutes meaning. Wright captures the danger of making human experience the vanguard of biblical interpretation; his strong words of caution deserve our attention:

70. Rose, *Sharing the Word*, 106.
71. Vanhoozer, *Is There a Meaning in This Text?*, 161–65.
72. Richard B. Hays, "Salvation by Trust? Reading the Bible Faithfully," *Christian Century*, February 1997, 18.

"Experience" is far too slippery for the concept to stand any chance of providing a stable basis sufficient to serve as an "authority," unless what is meant is that, as the book of Judges wryly puts it, everyone should simply do that which is right in their own eyes. . . . If "experience" is itself a *source* of authority, we can no longer be *addressed* by a word which comes from beyond ourselves. At this point, theology and Christian living cease to be rooted in God himself, and are rooted instead in our own selves; in other words, they become a form of idolatry in which we exchange the truth about God for a human-made lie. This, or something like it, is what we find with the popular modern varieties of Gnosticism, in which the highest religious good is self-discovery and then being "true" to the self thus discovered. But to elevate that imperative (now radically challenged by postmodernity, though this is not usually noticed in the relevant discussions) to the supreme status now claimed for it is to take a large step away from all known forms of orthodox Christianity.[73]

If the Bible is stripped of its freedom to speak a word from beyond us, then biblical interpretation and preaching are reduced to a clamor of our voices crying out from the situatedness of our creaturely experience.

Third, the problem of elevating the authority of the ecclesial community over the Bible is this: the assumption that there is safety in community is simply not true. Interpretation is no more sound and legitimate because it is pieced together with others. Vanhoozer turns this assumption on its head when he says, "The church's interpretation is to be preferred because it is *right—in accordance with the Scriptures*—not simply because it comes from the church."[74] In contrast to McClure's claim that the meaning and validity of the Bible are determined by its "linguistic and communicative use in the largest possible context,"[75] the truthfulness of Scripture rests not on people's responses to it but instead on God's own nature revealed in the Old and New Testaments and through the ministry of the Holy Spirit, who continues to testify about Christ (John 14:26; 15:26; 16:13–14; Rom. 8:15–16; Gal. 4:6; 1 John 5:6, 7–10). In other words, the church's experience of the Word is not an independent, determining factor in

73. N. T. Wright, *The Last Word: Beyond the Bible Wars to a New Understanding of the Authority of Scripture* (New York: HarperSanFrancisco, 2005), 102–3.
74. Vanhoozer, *Drama of Doctrine*, 164 (emphasis added).
75. McClure, *Other-Wise Preaching*, 102.

interpretation but rather should be considered in conjunction with and in light of Scripture and the Spirit's ongoing witnessing.

Even our best exegetical intentions and intuitions can be misled by pride, self-serving interests, and dynamics of power and politics. This is why we need the guardrails of the "rule of faith" and the "analogy of faith": we seek to understand Scripture in accordance with the core content of the apostles' teachings (rule of faith) and consider the unity and harmony of the whole Bible so that unclear passages are illuminated by easily understood passages (analogy of faith). Along with these, trust in the integrity and ability of our communicating God is the compass that allows us to take bold steps even when our hermeneutical path is unknown. Above all, the Holy Spirit who bears witness through and to Scripture in our hearts and in the world guides us and grants us sure footing.

As conversational preachers point out, the pulpit plays a vital role in fostering countercultural faith communities that embody love, solidarity, equality, and hospitality for *others*. To do so, the pulpit's uniqueness needs to be maintained, which means we must preserve the freedom and authority of Scripture to speak to us, for us, and even *against* our ways and experiences as a distinct word from God. Otherwise, Christian preaching begins to resemble the press, which P. T. Forsyth describes as having no "claim to anything but external freedom of opinion and expression" and having no "message as to whom the acting public must obey and trust."[76] What makes Christian preaching unique is the source of communication: Holy God, who through the Scriptures makes a decisive claim on us.

Every interpretative act and sermon preached is a choice about how we understand our relationship to Scripture: Is what we seek to do a *ministry* or an act of *mastery*? The apostles of the early church described the act of studying, understanding, and sharing the gospel of Jesus Christ as "the *ministry* of the Word" (Acts 6:4). Of all the contemporary depictions of preaching available, this stuffy word may seem too boring and unimaginative, but it nonetheless offers a vital reminder that interpretation and preaching exist to *serve* Scripture, not to *master* it by making it subservient to our needs, desires, and opinions.

76. P. T. Forsyth, *Positive Preaching and the Modern Mind* (New York: Armstrong & Son, 1907), 43.

Rethinking the Preacher's *Modus Operandi*: The Hermeneutic of Suspicion and the Hermeneutic of Faith

In light of what has been discussed so far concerning the problems of the conversational homiletic, this chapter closes by cautioning against using the hermeneutic of suspicion as the dominant approach to reading texts. I propose instead the need for coupling the hermeneutic of suspicion with the hermeneutic of faith, which restores meaning to the text.[77] The hermeneutic of suspicion is not anathema; when properly applied, it can "clear the horizon for a more authentic word, for a new reign of Truth, not only by means of a 'destructive' critique, but by the invasion of an art of interpreting."[78] On its own, however, this mode of reading has the potential to devolve to "the hermeneutic of alienation,"[79] in which texts perceived as offensive are rejected by interpreters as "the matters of truth and knowledge become translated as matters of power and privilege."[80]

What, then, is the proper place for the hermeneutic of suspicion? The hermeneutic of suspicion must work concertedly with the hermeneutic of faith. It is the dialectic of these polarities that sustains "double motivation" in biblical hermeneutics, which is the "willingness to suspect, willingness to listen; vow of rigor, vow of obedience."[81] David Lose traces a similar vein of thought when he writes: "The Christian interpreter and preacher simultaneously *trust* that God speaks through the Biblical witness even while admitting—nay, expecting—that God's speech comes through human speech and therefore always suffers the incompleteness of human perception and distortion of human sin."[82]

Being guided by the hermeneutic of trust means at least three things: First, every interpretive endeavor must begin with trust in God, who speaks through Scripture, and an approach to his Word with an open heart. Second, we need to apply the hermeneutic of suspicion foremost to ourselves so that, by God's grace, we can discern what Scripture is saying to us. And third, we must go beyond merely interpreting the Bible to actually

77. Ricoeur, *Freud and Philosophy*, 26–27. See also Lose, *Confessing Jesus Christ*, 138.
78. Ricoeur, *Freud and Philosophy*, 33.
79. Leander E. Keck, *The Church Confident* (Nashville: Abingdon, 1993), 59–65.
80. Vanhoozer, *Is There a Meaning in This Text?*, 372.
81. Ricoeur, *Freud and Philosophy*, 27.
82. Lose, *Confessing Jesus Christ*, 139.

living it out as was intended.[83] A faithful interpretation holds in tension the hermeneutic of suspicion and the hermeneutic of trust by recognizing God as the holy *Other* whom the church encounters in the Scriptures.[84] As Charles Bartow says, "Divinity has total freedom to act as itself, to disclose itself, to name itself, whereas human beings . . . have only limited freedom to do so." Interpreters thus need the humility to recognize that "it is not human beings who create God in their own image" but "the 'divine community,' God the Father, Son, and the Holy Spirit, [that creates] humanity in *its* own image."[85] Ministers must model an ethical interpretation that will "guard the otherness of the text" by preserving "its ability to say something to and affect the reader, thus creating the possibility of self-transcendence."[86]

Hence, every encounter with the Bible is laced with the question of whether we choose to respond with trust in God or out of fear of creaturely finitude. Nicholas Lash cites nihilism as a common human strategy used to deal with the "often bitter experience"[87] of life and the fragility and injustice of social constructions. In contrast to absolutism, which treats truth as unaffected by time and change, nihilism regards truth as a fictitious element that does not exist in reality but only in the space of human imagination and will. Irrespective of the differences between absolutism and nihilism, Lash notes that both are in the end "strategies of fear" that react to the finitude of human nature. In contrast to these strategies, the hermeneutic of faith and trust—or as Lash refers to it, "a strategy of trustfulness and not of terror"[88]—is the third option I will propose. Biblical hermeneutics is an exercise of faith in an infinite, all-powerful God—an exercise that takes a stand against fears of human limitations and failures. Faith is not only the hoped-for outcome of interpretation

83. Hays, "Salvation by Trust?," 220–22.

84. McClure also writes about reading Scripture in a way that preserves its transcendental quality of *otherness*. What differentiates his approach from what is described here is that McClure entrusts this task to the *community of human others* rather than to the *otherness of God*, which comes through the biblical text.

85. Charles Bartow, *God's Human Speech: A Practical Theology of Proclamation* (Grand Rapids: Eerdmans, 1997), 29–30.

86. Vanhoozer, *Is There a Meaning in This Text?*, 383.

87. Nicholas Lash, *Theology on the Way to Emmaus* (Eugene, OR: Wipf & Stock, 2005), 9–10.

88. Lash, *Theology on the Way to Emmaus*, 10.

and preaching; it is a requisite for both: "Believing in order to understand and understanding in order to believe."[89]

Thus the preacher's *modus operandi* for reading the Bible in the postmodern era or in any era should be faith in a communicating God. Faith is not only the most appropriate Christian response to postmodern skepticism and despair; the demonstration of faith in interpretation is also a powerful proclamation in and of itself about what we believe about God and what response befits those who encounter him in the revelation of Scripture. Although it is easy to focus our attention on the words we utter from the pulpit, the ministry of the Word must include proclamations of both explicit and implicit kinds (i.e., sermons as well as veiled attitude and stance toward God and Scripture) that equip the church to be competent readers of Scripture. The minister's posture before God's Word models for the congregation that God can be trusted. Richard Hays's words ring true: "We must consider how to read and teach Scripture in a way that opens up its message and both models and fosters *trust in God*. So much of the ideological critique that currently dominates the academy fails to foster these qualities. *Scripture is critiqued* but never interpreted. *The critic exposes but never exposits.* Thus the word itself recedes into the background, and we are left talking only about the politics of interpretation, having lost the capacity to *perform interpretations*."[90]

Conclusion

> O wonder!
> How many goodly creatures are there here!
> How beauteous [hu]mankind is! O brave new world,
> That has such people in't![91]

These iconic words are uttered by Miranda, the daughter of the wizard Prospero in Shakespeare's play *The Tempest*. Emerging out of her enclosed life on an island, Miranda exclaims with excitement when she encounters

89. Paul Ricoeur, *Figuring the Sacred: Religion, Narrative, and Imagination*, trans. David Pellauer, ed. Mark I. Wallace (Minneapolis: Fortress, 1995), 217.
90. Hays, "Salvation by Trust?," 222 (emphasis added).
91. Shakespeare, *The Tempest*, 5.1.184–87.

men who were brought there due to a shipwreck caused by a storm. The irony and naivety of her words become apparent against the backdrop of the story: the objects of her admiration included her father's usurpers who are responsible for banishing them to the island.

Aldous Huxley picks up the irony and captures it in the title of his novel *Brave New World*. In it, he depicts a dystopian society set in the future, where, despite all of its technological advances, the world is riddled by dysfunctions that signal the demise of humanity.[92] The world conjured up by Huxley is one that merely presents an illusion of a flourishing "new world" when, in reality, all is in decline.

As the church transitions from one era to another, preachers are compelled to search for new and progressive ways to understand the task of preaching in the awakening dawn of our brave new world. Conversational preaching is one proposal submitted in light of the cultural flux. This chapter investigated the latent claims and assumptions of the conversational model by setting it against the broad backdrop of postmodern epistemology. If the main strength of the conversational homiletic is the inclusion of the congregation's diverse perspectives in how the church understands Scripture, its greatest weakness is the inherent skepticism toward the Bible's communicative ability, which contrasts with trust in human construction of meaning. As this chapter concludes, Huxley's irony offers an important reminder: no matter how noble and dignified a community of human beings may appear to the eye, humankind is never as goodly or beauteous as we seem.

In contrast to Huxley's brave new world, Barth speaks about the "strange new world" of the Bible, which cannot be explained by history, morality, or religion but can begin to be understood only as the story of God that announces the "new beginning, out of which all things shall be made new."[93] To encounter that world, we must lean in with faith and "reach far beyond ourselves" because

> the Bible gives to every man [and woman] and to every era such answers to their questions as they deserve. We shall always find in it as much as we seek

---

92. Aldous Huxley, *Brave New World* (New York: Harper & Row, 1932).
93. Karl Barth, *The Word of God and the Word of Man*, trans. Douglas Horton (Gloucester, MA: Peter Smith, 1978), 41.

and no more: high and divine content if it is high and divine content that we seek; transitory and "historical" content, if it is transitory and "historical" content that we seek—nothing whatever, if it is nothing whatever that we seek. . . . The question, What is within the Bible? has a mortifying way of converting itself into the opposing question, Well, what are you looking for, and who are you, pray, who make bold to look?[94]

Hence, whatever else may be said of reading the Bible as Scripture, we most essentially must submit to God's sovereignty and humbly admit that humanity needs someone truly *other* than us to save us and free us from our sins of idolatry, prejudice, and injustice. The brave new world of the conversational homiletic appears to be teeming with resplendent interpretive possibilities, but it may not be as exquisite and prosperous if human subjectivity is the cornerstone of its construction.

Is it possible to draw on the strengths of the conversational homiletic while keeping its weaknesses in check? Can the traditional and conversational models of preaching balance each other constructively? Expressed differently, is it possible to preserve the identity of both the text and the reader? The next chapter explores these questions by looking at a dramatic approach that upholds the autonomy of the Bible to say and do what it intends without negating the church's creative engagement with it.

94. Barth, *Word of God*, 32.

4

A Dramatic Approach to Theology

Writing to disheartened believers in Thessalonica, the capital
of the Roman province of Macedonia, Paul uses a peculiar
expression at the beginning of his first letter that grounds
the rest of the writing: "And we also thank God constantly
for this, that when you received the word of God, which you heard from us,
you accepted it not as the word of men [and women] but as what it really
is, the word of God, which is at work in you believers" (1 Thess. 2:13).

These words capture an incredible hermeneutical unity shared by three
distinct agents of communication: God, messenger, and congregation.
Paul equates the words spoken by him and his ministry team with "what
it really is, the word of God," and their words are further linked to "the
word of God, which is at work in you believers." This auspicious picture
of the convergence of meaning and the harmony between the communicational agents that captured the hearts of the Reformers in the Second
Helvetic Confession turns the postmodern portrayal of language on its
head. The divine author is not pitted against readers, nor the preacher
against the congregation. Instead, these words suggest the real possibility of interpretive accord and of preaching as a faithful witness to the
ancient-yet-current Scriptures as God's Word without disregarding the
Spirit's ongoing missional work in the lives of congregation members.

The portrait of preaching glimpsed here provides the fulcrum for the homiletical model proposed in this book. To this end, this chapter turns to four theologians—Hans Urs von Balthasar, N. T. Wright, Nicholas Lash, and, primarily, Kevin Vanhoozer—who share Paul's confidence that hermeneutical unity between God, preacher, and congregation is possible and is, in fact, the grounds for thanksgiving in Christian fellowship. Yet these thinkers share more than interpretive optimism and geniality; they also speak with the same metaphoric language of drama as a conceptual framework for theology. This chapter highlights salient theological ideas of Balthasar, Wright, and Lash, which in many ways converge and expand in the robust theological vision of Vanhoozer. This overview accentuates various features of dramatic theology that address the extremes of the objectivism of the so-called *epic* theology and the pure subjectivism of *lyric* theology, which correspond respectively to the weaknesses of the traditional homiletic and those of the conversational homiletic. We then consider the deficiencies of epic and lyric modes of theology and preaching on their own and of the need for a third approach (i.e., dramatic) that can hold the contrapositions of epic and lyric in a dynamic tension that draws from their strengths.

Three Approaches to Theology: Epic, Lyric, and Dramatic

The concept of dramatic theology can be traced back to Hans Urs von Balthasar, who employed the terms *epic*, *lyric*, and *dramatic* to describe the common typologies of theology. Drawing from Hegel's ideas,[1] Balthasar applied these terms to theology in order to depict three different approaches to understanding faith,[2] although none "fit any actual theology or position precisely but yet [these approaches] illumine important tendencies."[3]

Theology and Preaching as Epic

Simply expressed, *epic* refers to a mode in which objectivity guides the theological endeavor. Epic "restrict[s] itself to grasping the historical

1. See G. W. F. Hegel, *Aesthetics: Lectures on Fine Art*, 2 vols., trans. T. M. Knox (Oxford: Clarendon, 1988).
2. Hans Urs von Balthasar, *Theo-drama: Theological Dramatic Theory*, vol. 2, *Dramatis Personae: Man in God* (San Francisco: Ignatius Press, 1990).
3. David F. Ford, *The Future of Christian Theology* (Oxford: Wiley, 2011), 25.

events as precisely as possible and describing them in their abiding 'universal significance.'"[4] When epic is the operative mode in engaging Scripture, theology takes on the form of a monologue (speech *about* God) that offers one overarching and comprehensive understanding of the biblical story. The theologian acts like an omniscient narrator who maintains a critical distance from the text in order to report historical events and facts with impartial clarity. This mode treats the Bible as a record of God's past actions, and theology as "the objective discussion of facts."[5] Such being the case, epic emphasizes the historicity of the Bible and tends to speak of God's works as already completed. Epic also privileges reason over feelings and deemphasizes "ambiguity, indirectness, irony, multi-leveled meaning, and multiple perspectives of characters, ideas, or events that do not seem to fit the movement toward a final resolution."[6] Scripture is conceptualized, and contextual particularities fade into the background in the epic mode. Therefore, the language of epic tends to be declarative and propositional, resembling a treatise or a council document[7] that makes all-encompassing claims.

The affinity between epic theology and the traditional homiletic is hard to miss. For example, one can detect epic notes in Haddon Robinson's well-known definition of preaching as "the communication of a biblical *concept*"[8] in which sermons take various forms—"an idea to be explained," "a proposition to be proved," "a principle to be applied," "a subject to be completed," or even "a story of Scripture [that] is narrated in such a way that the *idea* is developed directly or by implication."[9] According to

4. Balthasar, *Theo-drama*, 2:55.
5. Balthasar, *Theo-drama*, 2:57.
6. Ford, *Future of Christian Theology*, 24.
7. Balthasar, *Theo-drama*, 2:56.
8. Haddon W. Robinson, *Biblical Preaching: The Development and Delivery of Expository Messages*, 2nd ed. (Grand Rapids: Baker Academic, 2001), 35 (emphasis added).
9. Robinson, *Biblical Preaching*, 115–36 (emphasis added). Haddon Robinson's definitions apply to *expository* preaching. However, the word *expository* is omitted here to circumvent the limitation of the word. Broadly speaking, the expository approach is text-centered preaching that aims to affect listeners as the text once did for its original hearers. However, expository preaching has become more narrowly associated with particular philosophical and theological stances, which are the topic of investigation here. Since there are preachers who subscribe to the expository approach whose theological views align more closely with the dramatic approach (myself included), the term is left out to avoid the possible confusion that the preaching approach proposed in this work cannot be expository.

this view, preaching is primarily a systematic presentation of the Bible that helps people understand how to apply biblical truths to their lives. Like omniscient narrators in the epic mode, traditional preachers strive to maintain a critical distance from a passage they are studying. This allows them an objective, bird's-eye view of what is going on "without adding matter to the text that is not already there."[10] They have the "obligation" to "mine the text" fully—even "exhaust" the text. They exegetically analyze every part, leaving no significant aspect unexamined.[11] Once they grasp "the big idea," the proposition, or the basic principle in the text through a rigorous historical-critical study, knowledge is commonly communicated in a top-down style sermon that advances a general claim supported by specific conclusions that apply to listeners, often in the form of maxims, moral directives, or rules of conduct. In this, reason provides the constructive frame, and facts and concepts are the central building blocks for the sermon. The shape and style of sermons may vary, but the prevailing pattern is driven by an accurate report on and interpretation of the historical events and the bearing these have on listeners' lives. Preaching in the epic voice speaks a given word that rises from the historical events of God's interaction with humanity and summons the church to respond to what God has done. For this reason, the sermonic language tends to be instructional and delineative and to demand moral response.

Although we need the objectivity of epic, when epic is the sole operative mode, it leaves deficiencies in theology and preaching. Perhaps the greatest strength of epic is its ability to preserve the integrity of Scripture by submitting to the divine authorial intent. Epic grounds theology and preaching in the distinct good news of the Bible, which gives coherence and consistency to the biblical canon. We are reminded to listen to the text and pay attention to the story that it tells. The epic voice maintains that the Bible has a clear plot and the gospel has a recognizable propositional content and identifiable meaning that can be understood regardless of time and culture. As such, there are boundaries that distinguish Christian orthodoxy from heresy. However, a serious downfall of epic is its proclivity to reduce the multidimensional witness of the Scriptures to an absolute

10. Bryan Chapell, *Christ-Centered Preaching: Redeeming the Expository Sermon*, 2nd ed. (Grand Rapids: Baker Academic, 2005), 80.
11. Chapell, *Christ-Centered Preaching*, 118.

monologue, leaving little room for mystery, surprise, ambiguity, and dialogue. Epic "presumes a timeless perspective, which allows a privileged grasp and mastery of the whole [Scripture] in a detached stance of crude objectivity."[12] Also, a danger of epic is its tendency to treat the Bible as a solely historical book, overlooking the "not-yet" aspect in theology, which requires attentiveness to the Spirit's continuing work today. Theology and preaching in the epic mode can "encourage uncritical repetition" of the text and opt to retrieve and "rehearse the past" rather than being open to "new formulations"[13] of old truths, which encourage timely and fitting ways of embodiment in current contexts. Consequently, the epic voice alone fails to stir a deep and genuine sense of urgency in listeners to participate in God's ongoing initiatives and mission.[14]

Theology and Preaching as Lyric

In contrast to the objectivity of epic, lyric is guided by subjective self-expression. Unlike a neutral epic observer who values impartially, a lyric participant becomes intimately involved in the story. Lyric is the radical opposite of epic: "Whereas epic theology leaves no room for the present participation of the theologian in theology's subject matter, lyric theology . . . swings to the opposite extreme, virtually identif[ying] the subject matter of theology with the interpreter's religious experience."[15]

Lyric theology refers to "the internal motion of the devout subject, his [or her] emotion and submission, the creative outpouring of him[or her] self in the face of the vivid re-presentation, in its pristine originality, of what is past event."[16] Lyric gives primacy to inner feelings, moves, reflections, and experiences stirred by an individual's personal engagement with the biblical story ("prayer and personal involvement").[17] Given that priority, lyric theology aims to communicate the biblical story with enthusiasm, passion, and vivid imagination, making narratives come alive, as if they

12. D. C. Schindler, *Hans Urs von Balthasar and the Dramatic Structure of Truth: A Philosophical Investigation* (New York: Fordham University Press, 2004), 21.
13. Kevin Vanhoozer, *The Drama of Doctrine: A Canonical Linguistic Approach to Christian Theology* (Louisville: Westminster John Knox, 2005), 86.
14. Vanhoozer, *Drama of Doctrine*, 86.
15. Vanhoozer, *Drama of Doctrine*, 91.
16. Balthasar, *Theo-drama*, 2:55.
17. Balthasar, *Theo-drama*, 2:57.

are happening in the present moment. Another key difference between epic and lyric has to do with their engagement with time: "Lyric ignores time by reverting to atemporal subjectivity, while epic strives to overcome the contingency of time through imposing an artificial coherence."[18]

The impulses of lyric theology align with the proclivities of the conversational homiletic. Conversational preaching is inherently lyrical because its chief interest is to share the subjective experience of the community reading the Bible. To the proponents of the conversational homiletic, preaching is "a sort of *musing* process"[19] in which the church gathers around Scripture to *experience* it together and explore its impact on individual and communal lives. Disclosing biblical information is not the driving goal of conversational sermons. If facts, concepts, and principles mined from the Bible provide the building blocks of the traditional sermon, the basic components of the conversational sermon are collective impressions, affections, and passions fostered in the church's encounter with Scripture.

The conversational homiletic is also lyrical in that it celebrates manifold perspectives and experiences—even contradictions and tension points between them. It considers unequivocal knowledge impossible given the bias of human beings who can speak only from our own worldviews. Proponents of conversational preaching believe that the Word is "elusive" and "must be sought again and again in the multiplicity of biblical 'word images'" because "it is an incomprehensible Word this side of the eschaton with which we must engage in ongoing, relentless conversation."[20] So preaching can only be confessional and testimonial, like a tentative interpretation, proposal, or wager that represents at-the-moment formulations of what a biblical text means to particular people in a specific time and space.[21] The conversational homiletic embraces a lyrical fragmentation of truth and meaning unlike the traditional homiletic, which upholds epic coherence.

18. Samuel Wells, *Improvisation: The Drama of Christian Ethics* (Grand Rapids: Brazos, 2004), 49.

19. John S. McClure, *The Roundtable Pulpit: Where Leadership and Preaching Meet* (Nashville: Abingdon, 1995), 55.

20. Lucy Atkinson Rose, *Sharing the Word: Preaching in the Roundtable Church* (Louisville: Westminster John Knox, 1997), 103.

21. Rose, *Sharing the Word*, 100–101.

Furthermore, the conversational homiletic is lyrical because its theology and preaching are shaped by the church's *present* experience of Scripture. Conversational preachers believe that the Word is an "emergent communal reality"[22] that is always fluid because meaning takes form in the interchanges of people's reflections. Since meaning is emergent, Scripture is read in light of the church's ongoing experience of God's actions in the world today: "doctrines and meanings must be discerned and clarified through existential involvement."[23] That is to say, the experience of being in the world functions as a necessary lens to help read Scripture, and meaning continues to evolve for the church in the horizon of new encounters.

The lyric approach to theology and preaching has its advantages. Without lyric, theology and preaching become head matters that have no effect on the heart. The lyrical engagement allows the church not only to understand what Scripture is saying but also to experience it by participating in the world of the text. Lyric allows us to savor the immediacy of the biblical story, in all its glorious twists and turns, surprises, ironies, complexities, and tensions, rather than dissecting the story to death. In this sense, lyric also pushes theology and preaching away from an absolute monologue and shifts our attention to a chorus of voices that represent diverse viewpoints and experiences in the church. Lyric addresses the impossibility of epic: "The more one delves into the particularities of individual perspectives, conscious and subconscious motivations, rational and irrational responses, diverse worldviews, conditioning factors, hopes, fears, suspicions, doubts and desires, the less it seems that human reality can be done justice through an epic mindset."[24]

Nevertheless, the strong subjectivism of lyric needs to be kept in check. Lyric becomes problematic "insofar as its theologizing begins with one's own religious experience, [and it] neither recognizes nor responds to the prior word/act of the triune God."[25] The project of theology and preaching should not use the Bible to "corroborate human experience" but to "conform human experience to a word that precedes it."[26] In lyric, the

22. McClure, *Roundtable Pulpit*, 55.
23. Rose, *Sharing the Word*, 104.
24. Ford, *Future of Christianity*, 25.
25. Vanhoozer, *Drama of Doctrine*, 92.
26. Vanhoozer, *Drama of Doctrine*, 92.

boundaries that distinguish the gospel become fluid, and Christian theology and preaching become malleable to individual and communal preference and imagination. Moreover, a lyrical submersion in one's experience of Scripture does not allow a proper engagement with the full scope of God's actions in history. A real threat of lyric is theological myopia, which focuses only on what is immediately before us (e.g., how God is working in our personal lives, church, and local community) so that we fail to see a comprehensive picture of God's story that cuts across continents, cultures, and people groups. The point is, Scripture does tell a universal story that is true for all people at all times. Although we read the Bible *in light of our experience* in the world, it is critical that we also see our lives *in light of Scripture*. The danger of lyric is its tendency to neglect the latter by emphasizing the former. In the end, lyric on its own also does not elicit the church's true participation in God's mission in the world. Lyric turns to the contemplative, inner self to resist epic's imposed coherence on the external world. In this, the lyric mode of theology and preaching encourages "the self-expression of the subjective life" that "instead of proceeding to action remains alone with itself as inwardness."[27]

Theology as Dramatic: The Theodrama That Invites the Church's Participation[28]

What can bridge the chasm between the epic and the lyric modes of theology? How can the church preach the distinct gospel of Jesus Christ that has been made known to us, doing so with hermeneutical confidence and with humility that acknowledges our limitations and biases as knowers who live in a particular context? What can balance the extremes of the epic and the lyric?[29] How can preaching hold together the metanarrative of God's redemptive actions for the world with creative and particular expressions of human freedom?

According to Balthasar, the answer lies in drama. At its best, drama synthesizes epic and lyric in a way that brings together their strengths. The dramatic genre can steadily and coherently communicate the plot

---

27. Hegel, *Aesthetics*, 1038.

28. The next chapter will explore preaching shaped by dramatic theology in more depth.

29. Ben Quash, "'Between the Brutally Given, and the Brutally, Banally Free': Von Balthasar's Theology of Drama in Dialogue with Hegel," *Modern Theology* 13, no. 3 (1997): 293–318.

(i.e., epic) without sacrificing the complexity of diverse perspectives, motifs, themes, and ideas in a story (i.e., lyric). Drama traverses between epic and lyric in a way that neither advocates one's detachment from the story nor permits one to be drowned in the self-absorbed world of subjectivity. In its engagement with time, drama "celebrates and embraces an open and social future."[30] In drama "the *entire* person of the actor is laid claim to," so that "the living [person] is the material medium of expression."[31]

The notion of drama is significant for Balthasar because he believes that the Bible depicts a cosmic "theodrama" of God's redemptive words and actions that cannot be understood in either the epic or lyric mode alone. Central to Balthasar's theology is the belief that "the creation of the finite freedom by infinite freedom is the starting point of all theodrama."[32] The finitude of humanity manifests itself as endless restlessness in search for significance. Thankfully, however, humanity does not have to bear the burden of this predicament on our own, but we can choose to enter into a covenant relationship with the infinite God and participate in his continuing drama of salvation. Foundational to the theodrama is God's prior actions in initiating, creating, seeking out, saving, and commissioning human beings. In fact, this is precisely "what is at stake in theodrama . . . that God acts so as to take upon himself and make his own the tragedy of human existence even to the depths of that abyss."[33] From the very beginning, then, the theodrama is about God making room for humanity to join the fellowship of the Trinity. However, God's gracious initiatives and actions constitute the given plotline of the theodrama. "God's revelation is not an object to be looked at" with epic neutrality; "it is his action in and upon the world, and the world can only respond . . . through action on its part."[34] Through the sacrifice of God's Son—who exemplifies perfect obedience to the Father by submitting his freedom to the divine will—humanity is liberated to take part in God's drama. Human beings are not "doomed to play an endless succession of futile games with [ourselves] within [our]

---

30. Wells, *Improvisation*, 49.
31. Hegel, *Aesthetics*, 1039.
32. Balthasar, *Theo-drama*, 2:271.
33. Balthasar, *Theo-drama*, 2:54.
34. Hans Urs von Balthasar, *Theo-drama: Theological Dramatic Theory*, vol. 1, *Prolegomena* (San Francisco: Ignatius Press, 1989), 15.

own finitude."[35] Rather, Christ's death and resurrection allow us to stand on the world's stage with a God-given mission: "*En Christoi*, in the acting area Christ opens up as the fruit of his Resurrection, each individual is given a personal commission; he [or she] is entrusted both with something unique to do and with the freedom to do it."[36] Only when we participate in the theodrama by being "in Christ" do we find the true freedom to be uniquely ourselves. Divine initiation and human participation together is the key to Balthasar's understanding of the biblical theodrama and dramatic theology.

In sum, dramatic theology mends rifts in the opposing views of epic and lyric. For one, divine will and human freedom are subsumed in the theodrama that the church is called to faithfully and imaginatively enact. In other words, there are not two stories—ours and God's—that make sense of the world. Instead, the theodrama is the one story in which our individual and communal stories become the cosmic tale and find meaning and significance. As David Ford states,

> [In the Bible] there is no contradiction between divine purpose and initiative, on the one hand, and human freedom and responsibility, on the other. *Human freedom is fulfilled in involvement with God and God's purposes, and this means constant discernment of vocation and responsibility within an unfolding drama whose central act is the life, death, and resurrection of Jesus Christ.* This is an ongoing, irreducibly dramatic reality, and living within it requires alertness to God, other people, oneself, creation, and whatever is happening now, always looking toward the future of God's promising.[37]

Relatedly then, dramatic theology brings proposition and experience together as indispensable parts of a whole, which can then guide the church's involvement in God's ongoing drama. This symbiotic relationship between proposition and experience enriches our understanding of God and the mystery of God's work in Christ. Furthermore, dramatic theology discourages our attempts to artificially compartmentalize God's past, present, and future actions and instead gives God's story narrative unity and coherence.

---

35. Hans Urs von Balthasar, *Theo-drama: Theological Dramatic Theory*, vol. 3, *Dramatis Personae: Persons in Christ* (San Francisco: Ignatius Press, 1992), 50.
36. Balthasar, *Theo-drama*, 3:51.
37. Ford, *Future of Christian Theology*, 27 (emphasis original).

Scripture often demonstrates that God is not acting aimlessly, randomly, or haphazardly. Rather, God is like a skilled playwright who, with painstaking planning and artistic care, develops a narrative arc that builds toward an unfathomable climax and a glorious resolution. Scripture testifies about a Triune God who steadfastly commits to and enacts renewal in the world: the Father orchestrates history toward the climactic death and resurrection of his Son for the sake of the world; the Son goes to the cross in willing submission to the Father in order to carry out salvation for the world; and the Holy Spirit illumines and empowers the church to rightly participate in the new life of Christ by joining Christ's mission and moving toward the marvelous finale in the creation of a new heaven and earth.

The story we find ourselves part of is unified by the participation and performance of all three members of the Trinity and based on God's agency and action. So it is not enough for the church to know a scene or an episode in this story because this approach fragments "the Bible into bits—moral bits, systematic theological bits, devotional bits, historical-critical bits, narrative bits, and homiletical bits."[38] Dramatic theology puts before us a panoramic view of the full range of God's speech and events in history so that we can find our place in it and be taken up into its action. "Drama breaks out when the *subject* matter of theology (the epic component) reaches out and claims the self-involved (lyric) person. All of a sudden, revelation is demonstrated not to be a mere set of *past events* but a *present ferment*. All of a sudden, it becomes apparent that *one can have no real idea of the 'truth' of this revelation until one is caught up in it, relinquishing one's claim to neutrality*."[39]

N. T. Wright and Biblical Authority

Balthasar's concept of the theodrama parallels N. T. Wright's view of the Bible as a unifying thematic discourse.[40] Like Balthasar, Wright favors a dramatic view of Scripture that highlights the continuous actions

38. Michael W. Goheen, "The Urgency of Reading the Bible as One Story in the 21st Century" (lecture, Regent College, Vancouver, BC, November 2, 2006).
39. Ben Quash, "The Theo-drama," in *Cambridge Companion to Hans Urs von Balthasar*, ed. Edward T. Oakes and David Moss (New York: Cambridge University Press, 2004), 156 (emphasis added).
40. N. T. Wright, "How Can the Bible Be Authoritative?," *Vox Evangelica* 21 (1991): 7–32.

of God throughout history. Also like Balthasar, Wright believes that the performing God invites the church to the stage as co-performers in God's ongoing story. With regard to our discussion here, Wright's contribution shines the most in his elucidation of authority in relation to the Bible.

Wright compares the biblical story to a five-act Shakespearian play in which the fifth act has been lost. The first four acts are (1) creation, (2) fall, (3) Israel, and (4) Jesus. The fifth act opens with the New Testament stories of the earliest believers continuing what Jesus started in bringing God's kingdom to earth. The fifth act continues to include Christians in the present age, whose turn it now is to faithfully enact the gospel until the consummation of history, marked by Christ's return.[41] Although the script for the fifth act is "lost," Christians today need not fear or lose heart because we are not left without clues for how to carry on the story. We are given directions and guidelines for how to act our parts. The goal is not to repeat *ad infinitum* what has already been done in the first four acts, as that would not advance the story toward the eschatological conclusion (i.e., the epic tendency). Neither is it to discount or ignore what has been established by the playwright and what has happened thus far in the story, instead doing whatever feels right at the moment (i.e., the lyric tendency). The fitting Christian response according to Wright is "speaking and acting with both *innovation* and *consistency*."[42] In other words, we as Christian players should align our performance with the playwright's vision and intentions, respecting the boundaries set by the story line, themes, developments, and movement, even as we strive to creatively embody our roles in new performative contexts.

The script for the first four acts guides the performers in the fifth act. The first four acts supply a bounty of description about the plot and the

41. While appreciating Wright's theological model, Samuel Wells contests Wright's five acts because (1) the church taking up the last act of the play erroneously suggests that resolution hinges entirely on the church; (2) by placing the church in the final act, eschaton is only implicit, and thus this view does not sufficiently point to God as the one who brings the story to completion; (3) Jesus, who is the climax of the drama and the object of the New Testament witness, should be placed in act 3, at the center of the whole story; and (4) Wright's segmentation of creation and fall seems incongruent with Scripture's portrayal of these "inaugural" events that tell how human disobedience distorted God's gift of freedom. For these reasons, Wells modifies Wright's five-act play in the following way: (1) creation, (2) Israel, (3) Jesus, (4) church, and (5) eschaton. See Wells, *Improvisation*, 52–57.

42. Wright, "How Can the Bible Be Authoritative?," 18–19 (emphasis original).

necessary directions for actors to participate in the drama. Wright calls the power of this story that gives agency to actors and directs them to rightly participate in the drama *authority*. Biblical authority does not operate by a list of binding rules that disregards particularities and merely requires routinized obedience. Rather, the power Wright refers to is God's authority mediated through Scripture[43]—a kind of enabling power that makes the church in diverse contexts "live under the 'authority' of the extant story, being required to offer something between an improvisation and an actual performance of the final act."[44] Wright's view of biblical authority challenges both epic and lyric understandings because these understandings treat power either as something possessed by a single narrator or as an individual expression of freedom. According to Wright, it is precisely the power of story that enables the church to creatively embody the fifth act without sacrificing the story's substance or form.

Nicholas Lash and Communal Performance

Nicholas Lash also writes on the theme of the church's participatory performance in the ongoing divine drama, but he furthers the discussion by bringing special attention to the communal aspect of the performance.[45] Lash agrees with Balthasar and Wright that *performance* is the final goal of interpretation. Lash observes that distinct texts (e.g., a map, a poem) call for different actions (e.g., to follow the directions, to read). When it comes to the biblical text, the objective is not to contemplate ideals or prop up delusions; the *telos* of biblical hermeneutics is a performance that gives the text's meaning a living form. Scripture comes alive to the fullest extent only when those who are immersed in the biblical drama embody the script, straddling creative improvisation and fidelity to the otherness of the text. These should not be solitary assignments, but rather the reading and performance of the Scriptures are the mission of the *whole church*. Interpretation is a "collaborative enterprise" because we need "experts" who assist the church in understanding the biblical text and because the

43. N. T. Wright, *Scripture and the Authority of God: How to Read the Bible Today* (New York: HarperOne, 2011).

44. Wright, "How Can the Bible Be Authoritative?," 19.

45. Nicholas Lash, *Theology on the Way to Emmaus* (Eugene, OR: Wipf & Stock, 1986), 37–46.

nature of performance calls for a company of players to enact a text.[46] Lash's point does not minimize the personal responsibility of each interpretive performer. He suggests that personal responsibility should not be confused with "private judgment"—discerning and carrying out interpretive judgments that rely solely on one's own intellectual and experiential facilities.[47] Lash concludes that "the fundamental form of the *Christian* interpretation of scripture is the life, activity and organization of the believing community," and that "Christian practice, as interpretive action, consists in the *performance* of texts which are construed as 'rendering,' bearing witness to, one whose words and deeds, discourse and suffering, 'rendered' the truth of God in human history."[48]

Kevin Vanhoozer and Dramatic Theology

Sharing in the convictions of Balthasar, Wright, and Lash, Kevin Vanhoozer casts one of the most comprehensive pictures of theodramatic theology. He understands the task of Christian theology as providing sound doctrinal directions from the biblical canon for the church's faithful and creative performance in the ongoing theodrama. Vanhoozer develops a unique angle by engaging George Lindbeck's philosophical theology (and even taking cues from his cultural-linguistic approach) but rectifying Lindbeck's postliberalism by reorienting it to the tradition of *sola Scriptura*.

Rectifying George Lindbeck's theological vision. In his seminal work, *The Nature of Doctrine*,[49] Lindbeck draws from Clifford Geertz's cultural anthropology, Peter Berger's social theory, Ludwig Wittgenstein's linguistic turn in philosophy, and William A. Christian Sr.'s critical philosophy of religion. Taking these into account, Lindbeck suggests a "cultural-linguistic" view of culture, religion, and language.[50] Lindbeck describes a pernicious dichotomy in Western Protestantism between *cognitive-propositionalism*, which is associated with conservative evangelicals, and *experiential-expressivism*, which is associated with liberal Protestants.

46. Lash, *Theology on the Way to Emmaus*, 43.
47. Lash, *Theology on the Way to Emmaus*, 43.
48. Lash, *Theology on the Way to Emmaus*, 42 (emphasis original).
49. See George A. Lindbeck, *The Nature of Doctrine: Religion and Theology in a Postliberal Age* (Philadelphia: Westminster, 1984).
50. See also Hans Frei, *The Eclipse of Biblical Narrative: A Study in Eighteenth- and Nineteenth-Century Hermeneutics* (New Haven: Yale University Press, 1974).

These terms are reminiscent respectively of Balthasar's epic and lyric theologies and, for our purpose, of traditional and conversational models of preaching.

According to Lindbeck, both groups have misstepped in responding to questions generated by the Enlightenment. Chief among these blunders relates to hermeneutics and understanding the Bible in relation to revelation. Scholars from the conservative camp, such as Charles Hodge, are concerned with protecting scriptural authority in order to maintain the Bible's propositional nature and its function as a record of historical events (this concern shares an affinity with the traditional model of preaching). According to this view, doctrines are truth statements about objective reality. Conversely, the liberal camp, as represented by scholars like Friedrich Schleiermacher, emphasizes the reader's subjective experience as the truly meaningful component when evaluating the biblical text. Liberal theologians espouse the perspective that doctrines are expressions of the common human religious experience (this emphasis shares an affinity with the conversational model of preaching).

Unsatisfied by these polarizations, Lindbeck's cultural-linguistic approach finds an alternative solution in the church's practices and tradition. The core of his theological model contends that "the function of church doctrines . . . is their use, not as expressive symbols or as truth claims, but as communally authoritative rules of discourse, attitude, and action."[51] Doctrines merely act as the grammar of the language game that is played within Christianity. "Like a culture or language," Lindbeck asserts, religion "is a communal phenomenon that shapes the subjectivities of individuals rather than being primarily a manifestation of those subjectivities."[52] Becoming a Christian is "a process of socialization or enculturation within a particular cultural-linguistic community."[53] Christians learn to think, speak, and act by learning a set of rules that govern their lives in that community. As seen from this perspective, the Bible is best understood as both narrative and doctrine (i.e., a storied practice).

While Lindbeck uses the terms *cognitive-propositionalism* and *experiential-expressivism*, Vanhoozer uses the terms *epic* and *lyric* to discuss

---

51. Lindbeck, *Nature of Doctrine*, 18.
52. Lindbeck, *Nature of Doctrine*, 33.
53. Lindbeck, *Nature of Doctrine*, 33.

views of doctrine.[54] Although Vanhoozer agrees with Lindbeck on the insufficiencies of these approaches to theology, Vanhoozer is not so quick to dismiss the two perspectives. In fact, he proposes "to rehabilitate the cognitive-propositional approach to theology by expanding what we mean by 'cognitive' and by dramatizing what we mean by 'proposition.'" Identifying the mishap in Lindbeck's thinking by reducing what is "cognitive" to the literal and static, Vanhoozer echoes Paul Ricoeur when he refers to metaphors as an example of "the properly cognitive nature of nonliteral language," in which words "are not susceptible to literal paraphrase, not because they are noncognitive but because they have a *surplus* of cognition."[55] He asserts that epic theology fails when it divorces the

54. Given that terms like *cognitive-propositionalism, experiential-expressivism, cultural linguistics*, as well as *epic* and *lyric*, are linguistic markers that represent philosophical and theological stances, it is clear that all the characteristics of the conversational homiletic cannot be captured by one or more of these labels. Notwithstanding the danger of oversimplification, it is beneficial to note that the homiletic model advocated by Lucy Rose, John McClure, and O. Wesley Allen Jr. has elements of experiential-expressivism and postliberalism in its hermeneutical essence. The conversational homiletic is emblematically lyric (or as Lindbeck would call it, experiential-expressivism), with its strong emphasis on the reader's subjective experience of the text. At the same time, conversational homiletic is also postliberal. This is clear from the name O. Wesley Allen Jr. has chosen for his preaching model ("ecclesial collaborative homiletic") and his portrayal of preaching as "language lessons" in which a community acquires the necessary vocabulary for the language game of religion. At a glance, the term *postliberal* may seem less descriptive of preaching as promoted by Lucy Rose and John McClure because the voices of those from the margins are the linchpin of their homiletical models rather than the voices of existing communities (which have routinely constituted the ecclesial tradition). Both McClure and Rose promote a centrifugal approach to theology and, relatedly, to preaching, where preachers must step beyond the boundaries of their traditional ecclesial communities to encounter "others" who ought to be included in the church's hermeneutical and homiletical table conversations. This form of de-centering from the common traditions of the church in order to welcome those on the fringes may appear contrary to postliberalism and its stress on the existing central practices of the church. However, McClure's and Rose's understanding of preaching is still postliberal at its core because language is regarded as a product of a self-referential symbol system that is religion, and they emphasize the use of Scripture and its function in an ecclesial community.

Although McClure and Rose resist the association of postliberalism by advocating a turn to the faceless ideals of *others* in theory, on a practical level, their preaching models still center on the people in their own communities and the interpretive use of Scripture in their familiar practices. If ecclesial pluralism is the interest of McClure's and Rose's homiletical projects, such crosscontextual and crosscultural conversations can still take place, even "while standing in [our traditions]" as long as the members of the community are open to critical dialogues (see J. Wentzel van Huyssteen, *Essays in Postfoundationalist Theology* [Grand Rapids: Eerdmans, 1997], 38). Since conversationalists view language as a product of a self-referential symbol system and emphasize the *use* of Scripture and its *function* in an ecclesial community, they share more in common with postliberal thinking than they might admit.

55. Vanhoozer, *Drama of Doctrine*, 88 (emphasis original).

truthful content of Scripture from its concrete uses. The dramatic nature of the gospel resists being reduced to such axiomatic use.

Embracing the position of a critical realist,[56] Vanhoozer affirms that a determinate meaning and a sound interpretation of the text do indeed undergird the propositional content of the scriptural message: "The gospel *does* inform: 'He is risen.' Without this propositional core, the church would be evacuated of its raison d'être, leaving only programs and potlucks. To deny a propositional component to theology is in effect 'an attack on the notion of revealed religion.'"[57]

As a critical realist, however, Vanhoozer equally asserts that interpretation is a dialectic act of appropriation that weighs others' perspectives with the humility of one who has not obtained the finality of meaning. By his own admission, Vanhoozer's hermeneutical stance is thus best construed as *pluralist, inclusivist*, and *exclusivist*.[58] As a *pluralist* he values sundry perspectives that constitute the "thick" description that a theologian must fairly take into consideration in the act of interpretation. He is an *inclusivist* because he holds to the belief that "one determinate meaning encompasses more than one level of description." He is an *exclusivist* because he strives to discover and adhere to the "one determinate meaning" of Scripture that is sound.[59]

Lindbeck's cultural-linguistic model takes a step in the right direction by proposing a narrative view of Scripture that avoids dichotomizing the Bible either as an encoded archive of propositions or as a mirror that merely reflects the subjectivities of its readers. Nevertheless, Lindbeck's misjudgment comes in turning to the ecclesial tradition as the supreme authority that legitimizes and governs the interpretation of Scripture. Tradition is essential and indispensable to hermeneutics, but it should not supplant Scripture as the norm by which all doctrines and practices

56. J. Wentzel van Huyssteen describes the position of critical realism in theology as making "a proposal about the provisionality, but also the reliability, of our theological knowledge. Without losing the validity of the fact that all of our knowledge is always socially contextualized, critical realists—with good reasons, but not on compelling grounds—claim reference for their tentative proposals." Van Huyssteen, *Essays in Postfoundationalist Theology*, 43.

57. Vanhoozer, *Drama of Doctrine*, 91. Here, Vanhoozer quotes from Colin Gunton, *A Brief Theology of Revelation* (Edinburgh: T&T Clark, 1997), 7.

58. Kevin J. Vanhoozer, *Is There a Meaning in This Text? The Bible, the Reader, and the Morality of Literary Knowledge* (Grand Rapids: Zondervan, 1998), 301–2.

59. Vanhoozer, *Is There a Meaning in This Text?*, 302.

are measured and assessed. In the same way that cultures are not "closed systems, insular and internally consistent wholes that preserve a stable deposit of values and knowledge,"[60] Vanhoozer argues that ecclesial cultures do not hold the final jurisdiction in determining the meaning of Scripture. The reality of the church's "eclectic" tradition that spans vast time and distance further exacerbates this doubt. Since cultures are porous entities in constant flux and influenced by multiple factors, we cannot boil down the diversity of ecclesial tradition into one form or somehow extricate one "superior" set of practices from the others. Herein lies a major problem in Lindbeck's cultural-linguistic model:

> If it is not possible to identify a stable core of Christian practice, then it is hard to see how church practice can serve as a norm. Though Lindbeck claims that Christians learn how to speak and act and think as Christians by participating in the church's form of life, "there is no non-circular way of specifying who the competent players are." Neither is there an easy way to abstract a stable set of rules from the many forms of Christian practice or to apply the same set of rules to different, often messy cultural situations: "Appeal to communal norms will not guarantee, then, as postliberals want it to, stability underneath the changing forms of history."[61]

We are interpreters formed by tradition; we stand in the fertile soil of accumulated wisdom, creeds, confessions, and practices of the church, which have been passed down through history, and we read Scripture as members of that wider ecclesial community. By the work of the Spirit, who works through the God-breathed Scripture, we all share beliefs and habits of mind and body that unite us in our faith as the body of Christ. Vanhoozer is not dismissing the "rule of faith" as a critical parameter for biblical interpretation. He is suggesting neither a bifurcation of tradition and Scripture nor emancipation from all those traditions and practices that profoundly shape who we are. He does, however, reprioritize what constitutes authority in biblical interpretation by naming Scripture as the "norming norm."

60. Vanhoozer, *Drama of Doctrine*, 121.
61. Vanhoozer, *Drama of Doctrine*, 121. Here, Vanhoozer quotes from Kathryn Tanner, *Theories of Culture* (Minneapolis: Fortress, 1997), 141–42.

Doctrine as dramatic: A canonical-linguistic approach. So where should the church turn to understand the Bible? Vanhoozer advances a new theological framework in his "canonical-linguistic approach" that clings to the scriptural canon instead of the ecclesial tradition as the authority in biblical interpretation. Rejecting theology as epic, lyric, or storied practice, Vanhoozer sets forth a vision of theology as dramatic.[62] Echoing the voices of Balthasar, Wright, and Lash, Vanhoozer promotes Scripture as a five-act divine discourse. Since the theodrama is about *God's actions*, each act should be thought of as "a vital ingredient in the historical outworking of the divine decree" that together make up these five acts: (1) creation, (2) electing Abraham, (3) sending the Son, (4) sending of the Spirit, and (5) return of the King.[63] In this divine drama, "the Father is the playwright and producer of the action; the Son is the climax and summation of the action. . . . The Spirit, as the one who unites us to Christ, is the dresser who clothes us with Christ's righteousness, the prompter who helps us remember our biblical lines, and the prop master who gives gifts (accessories) to each church member, equipping us to play our parts."[64]

Scripture, then, is a script intended for live performance by the church, not "an authoritative script that calls merely for intellectual assent."[65] The Bible exists for the community of believers to interpret the drama

62. In prior decades, works like Hans Frei's *The Eclipse of Biblical Narrative* have contributed significantly to biblical and theological studies, not least by employing the category of narrative to recast theological convictions of Scripture. More generally, narrative has been recognized as a useful trope to describe the storied existence of human beings and even to depict how congregational cultures preserve their identities and engage a storied society. More recently, however, narrative has come under some criticism as an inadequate model for theology. Kevin Vanhoozer identifies three primary deficiencies. First, given that there are multiple biblical accounts that attest to even one historical event, the notion of "*the* biblical narrative" is misleading. Second, narrative erodes Scripture's richness by collapsing many genres into a single form. Third, the primary shortcoming of narrative is that it does not invite participation because it doesn't make the church's role as explicit as it could be in the gospel story. Vanhoozer asserts that *drama* supplements what is lacking in narrative theology by recognizing the pluriformity of the biblical text and by inviting the church to be active participants of the ongoing theodrama (Vanhoozer, *Drama of Doctrine*, 273). See also Thomas Long's critique of narrative preaching in *Preaching from Memory to Hope* (Louisville: Westminster John Knox, 2009), and Paul Ricoeur's critique of narrative theology in "Toward a Narrative Theology: Its Necessity, Its Resources, Its Difficulties," in *Figuring the Sacred: Religion, Narrative, and Imagination* (Minneapolis: Fortress, 1995), 236–48.

63. Vanhoozer, *Drama of Doctrine*, 98. This division of the play is similar to N. T. Wright's, but, like Samuel Wells, Vanhoozer does not consider the fall of humanity to be a separate act.

64. Vanhoozer, *Drama of Doctrine*, 448.

65. Vanhoozer, *Drama of Doctrine*, 236.

of redemption in two senses: (1) "the script records and makes sense of the divine action in the past," and (2) "the script solicits the interpreter's participation in the ongoing action in the present."[66] In fact, Vanhoozer's dramatic approach to theology seeks to do precisely this: to bridge the long-severed relationship between *orthodoxy* (right belief) and *orthopraxis* (right/wise practice) with *orthokrisis* (right judgment).[67] Training the church to develop an "imagination that corresponds to and continues the gospel by making good theological judgments about what to say and do in light of the reality of Jesus Christ" is the critical role of theology, as he sees it.[68]

Concerning the role of Scripture in the theodrama, Vanhoozer offers strong words of admonition and encouragement. He warns that since the Bible communicates God's action, the text's freedom to say and do things must be preserved. This is not to say that interpreters are enslaved to the text, but that the theodramatic plot provides clear constraints and guidelines for our interpretive freedom. The text's ontology determines how we ought to read and interpret it. Therefore we would do well to align ourselves with what God (the divine author who works through human writers) is saying and doing through Scripture, which corresponds with its nature, purpose, and function as he designed it. Vanhoozer contends, "Though other interpretive interests are legitimate, . . . to go wrong here—in describing what authors were saying/doing—is to miss the very raison d'être of the text."[69] To describe the right posture of Christian interpreters, he uses the image of martyrs, who surrender their sense of self to divine wisdom, will, and plan.[70] From this perspective, the goal of theological hermeneutics moves from mere mastery to "a matter, first, of grasping the basic plot—of being able to relate the various scenes in the theodrama to what God has done climactically in Jesus Christ—and, second, of grasping how we can go on following Christ in new situations

66. Kevin Vanhoozer, "Imprisoned or Free? Text, Status, and Theological Interpretation in the Master/Slave Discourse of Philemon," in *Reading Scripture with the Church: Toward a Hermeneutic for Theological Interpretation*, ed. A. K. M. Adam, Stephen E. Fowl, Kevin Vanhoozer, and Francis Watson (Grand Rapids: Baker Academic, 2006), 73.

67. Vanhoozer, *Drama of Doctrine*, 30.

68. Vanhoozer, *Drama of Doctrine*, 30.

69. Vanhoozer, "Imprisoned or Free?," in Adam, Fowl, Vanhoozer, and Watson, *Reading Scripture with the Church*, 61.

70. Vanhoozer, *Drama of Doctrine*, 133.

so that our speech and action correspond to the truth of the gospel."[71] Herein lies the encouragement for the church: Scripture can be read with confidence because it "has determinate content."[72]

What, then, is the preacher's role in the theodrama? Vanhoozer answers: "While the Holy Spirit is the primary director who oversees the global production, it is the pastor who bears the primary responsibility for overseeing local performances."[73] Collaborating with theologians, who are dramaturges, pastor-directors have the responsibility to "come up with a unified vision embracing both the drama (with the author's entire creative contribution) and the art of actors (with their very different creative abilities)."[74] This translates into a twofold duty for pastor-directors: (1) to ensure that the team soundly understands the script within the boundaries established by the playwright, and (2) to train actors not only as individuals but also as a theater company to stand with a unified vision for performing the theodramatic action. The pastor-director participates not just as another member of the congregation who tosses out one among myriad interpretations of the Bible. As the preacher remains attentive to the voices of those in the congregation, the preacher's primary responsibility is also to proclaim the gospel faithfully in all areas of ecclesial life with humble confidence. The assurance and authority of the preacher derive not from certitude and hierarchical power but instead from faith in the truthfulness of a communicating God who is still at work among his people and in the world today.

It is noteworthy that the pastor's role of "directing" should not be confused with "dictating."[75] Just as a skilled director helps actors immerse themselves fully in a story so that they can rise up from it and creatively bring the script to life through improvisation, ministers train believers to be competent Christian performers who can skillfully embody the roles assigned to them in their contexts. Captivation with the gospel (theodramatic) reality finds tangible form in Christian performance. Vanhoozer explains: "The primary task of the director, after helping people to understand the play, is to help each player grow into his or her part. This is largely a matter

71. Vanhoozer, "Imprisoned or Free?," in Adam, Fowl, Vanhoozer, and Watson, *Reading Scripture with the Church*, 77.
72. Vanhoozer, *Drama of Doctrine*, 448.
73. Vanhoozer, *Drama of Doctrine*, 448.
74. Balthasar, *Theo-drama*, 1:298; quoted in Vanhoozer, *Drama of Doctrine*, 448.
75. Vanhoozer, *Drama of Doctrine*, 448.

of enabling the players to see their identity as 'in Christ,' and perhaps of criticizing mechanical acting. The pastor helps the congregation become better actors by helping them learn the script and understand how it should be performed in the present cultural sense."[76] The gospel invites all who are redeemed to be part of a company of "costumed interpreters"[77] called the church.

Vanhoozer refers to the works of Lindbeck and others who focus on the actions of the believing community over the communicative action of the Triune God as second-level interpretation, or "performance II interpretation." This kind of performance rises out of a fallacious view that confuses the church's interpretive role with that of authoring and directing the biblical script. He distinguishes such erroneous practice from what he refers to as "performance I interpretation," which is "a matter not of authoring but of 'answerability,' of *acknowledging* what the playwright is doing in the many voices in Scripture and of *responding* to it in an appropriate manner."[78] Vanhoozer maintains that performance I interpretation is what the church should strive to enact. The church is "a company of players gathered together to stage scenes of the kingdom of God for the sake of the watching world."[79] Adopting David Scott's view on interpretation, Vanhoozer asserts:

> It is only as a company that the people of God can function as a "hermeneutic of the gospel": "Interpretation may be so institutionalized in schools and done by learned men and women that it has become over-identified with ideas and written commentaries. . . . The most authentic Christian biblical interpretation is human enactments of God-informed life. . . . Interpretation, then, in its final form, is God-formed human practice. What we do as the people of God is our interpretations of the Bible." The theater of the gospel requires not only a priesthood but a *playerhood* of all believers in which every member of the church plays an important role.[80]

76. Vanhoozer, *Drama of Doctrine*, 449.
77. Vanhoozer, *Drama of Doctrine*, 413.
78. Vanhoozer, *Drama of Doctrine*, 180 (emphasis original).
79. Vanhoozer, *Drama of Doctrine*, 32.
80. Vanhoozer, *Drama of Doctrine*, 413–14 (emphasis original). Vanhoozer quotes from David Scott, "Speaking to Form: Trinitarian-Performative Scripture Reading," *Anglican Theological Review* 77 (1995): 144–45. Vanhoozer credits the expression "hermeneutic of the gospel" to Lesslie Newbigin.

Of course one cannot deny that the ecclesial community—the story of *us*—is essential to Christianity. Nonetheless, Vanhoozer reminds us that prior to the story of us is the story of the One and Only, and it is in his drama that the fragmented and broken stories of our lives and communities find meaning and wholeness. If the church replaces biblical authority, nothing remains to confront the church's own fallibility. Thus, even against the malpractice of the church, the Bible's freedom to speak prophetically must be preserved (i.e., to name human sins, announce divine judgment and grace). The church, after all, is not an interpretation of itself but a "lived interpretation of Scripture."[81]

Conclusion

From the perspective of dramatic theology, we understand the Bible as a masterful script of cosmic proportion with God as the playwright, the main actor, and the producer, who continues on his mission to bless and renew all creation. Seeing the Bible as such a script has profound implications for preaching. First, it is not enough that we understand or experience what the Bible says in preaching because the Bible must be *lived out* and *performed* in the world. Scripture provides the directions for the church's "live-action" in the continuing drama of redemption that God graciously invites us to participate in. So our concern in preaching should not be strictly epic oriented because sermons should do more than accurately report God's historical actions, although faithful witnessing and testifying are no doubt vital components. At the same time, sermons should not be purely lyrical because affections stirred by personal and communal experiences of God are not an end in themselves but are pathways that take us to a world that needs to "taste and see that the LORD is good" (Ps. 34:8). We need both epic and lyric in order to effectively perform the biblical drama that makes God's grace and truth known to the world.

Second, if preachers see the Bible as a divine script, they can have confidence that the theodramatic plot has a discernible, unifying meaning. The theodrama is not amorphous and open-ended. The story line of God's faithful actions in history conveys distinctly good news about

81. Vanhoozer, *Drama of Doctrine*, 349.

God's covenantal love and goodness. This message is revealed in the person of Jesus Christ, the Word, who is God (see John 1:1). Far from being bereft of meaning, then, the theodrama of Scripture abounds with laws, commands, exhortations, promises, stories, songs, and pictures that teach us about God, his will, and his plan to bless all creation. The invitation extended to all calls us to inhabit a *particular* world that is described and endorsed in the biblical script: the reality of being "in Christ," which differs radically from operating within the world's narratives. A dramatic theological framework for preaching offers an important corrective to the conversational homiletic by contending not only that the reality made available through Christ is recognizable and knowable from the Bible but also that the primordial matter of preaching is to be subservient both to the playwright's vision for what that reality looks like and to his will to make *that* reality known above all else.[82]

Third, the analogy of the Bible as a script opens up imaginative space for preaching to responsibly explore diverse renderings of what it means for the church to enact the theodrama in different contexts. This implication balances the previous point. The theodrama communicates a distinct and significant story that relates to the lives and eternity of all people in all places and times. However, this communication does not rule out creative freedom for the players who enact the biblical script in the shifting horizon of culture. The players are not subsumed into the theodrama, stripped of their individual uniqueness and enslaved to the weight of its rigidity. This is precisely the danger of the traditional homiletic that has been discussed in the earlier chapters: construing truth as being one dimensional, as if there is one absolute way of living it out. The "truth" that the Bible portrays is not a fixed concept to be grasped but the person of Jesus Christ, with whom we have a relationship (John 14:6). Hence Christian performance

---

82. Concerning the trend in performance arts to displace authors from the process of production, Jean Luere notes: "The author . . . whose creative imagination was once considered the validating source of all art, was finally sent to the guillotine." See Jean Luere, ed., "Literary Assumptions about Text," in *Playwright versus Director: Authorial Intentions and Performance Interpretations* (Westport, CT: Greenwood Press, 1994), 6. This haunting thought applies to preaching today as well. It demands that preachers consider whether "literature that has been stripped of any positive value" is "worth reading and interpreting, let alone, performing" (6; Luere quotes from Alvin Kernan, *The Death of Literature* [New Haven: Yale University Press, 1990], 213).

seeks to keep the "constancy and the development of character"[83] with the rest of the theodrama in light of who Jesus is so that there is *coherence* and *consistency* to the story we enact.

This chapter began by asking whether interpretive harmony between God, the preacher, and the congregation is possible. This chapter closes by asserting that interpretive harmony is not only achievable but also a tenable goal for preaching.

Rather than surrendering to postmodern despair and disillusionment regarding language and authority, preaching best operates from trust in God's communicative ability to speak to the church and via the church to the world through the primary means of Scripture and its theodrama. It can operate thus because the gospel has a distinguishable shape and identifiable propositional content that has a unifying meaning. Biblical authority is the power of the extant story to liberate the church to be what we are meant to be in Christ. A dramatic view of Scripture with God as the author (Father), actor (Son), and director (Spirit) empowers the church to cling to the uniqueness of the gospel, even as we celebrate diverse performative renderings of what it means to be "in Christ" in many different contexts.

Preaching does not have to impose an artificial, monolithic view of truth veiled as interpretive harmony. Nor does the playwright's vision have to be pitted against the church's ongoing experience in the world. The biblical script grounds, enlightens, inspires, affirms, and keeps accountable the church's enactment of the gospel in the world. In this way the theodrama is able to steadily hold together proposition and experience, coherence and particularity, and divine action and human participation. Preaching's integral task is to help believers see the truth of the theodrama, find their parts in it, and animate them to act in ways that correspond to God's intent, will, and plan. In this way, preaching enables believers to participate in the future that only God could have envisioned and that only God brings about.

Again, Paul seems to know this when he writes his first letter to the Thessalonian church. He appeals to the coherence and consistency of trinitarian action as the ground for his thanksgiving in 1 Thessalonians

---

83. Wells, *Improvisation*, 60. See also Walter Brueggemann, *The Bible and the Postmodern Imagination: Texts under Negotiation* (London: SCM, 1993).

2:13. He writes, "And we also thank God constantly for this, that when you received the word of God, which you heard from us, you accepted it not as the word of [humans] but as what it really is, the word of God." The preached word that testifies to the past faithfulness of God, especially as revealed and fulfilled in the death and resurrection of Jesus Christ, is the same word of God that is dynamically and actively at work in the Thessalonians by the Spirit's ongoing ministry.

Paul teaches the Thessalonians that as ones who have heard and received the word of God as it really is, they are now part of a larger story. This story tells of a greater kingdom than Rome and of their destinies—not for wrath but for salvation through Jesus Christ (1 Thess. 5:9). Nonetheless, they will encounter persecution and hostility from those who "displease God and oppose all [hu]mankind" (2:15). In response to such antagonists in the story, Paul instructs the Thessalonians to not be surprised by hostility but instead to be steadfast in their faith by living a life of purity and love that pleases God (4:1–12); after all, they stand in the lineage of Jesus, Judean Christians, the prophets, and Paul and his ministry partners (2:14–15).

All who believe in Jesus Christ have reason to hope because we know the story's end: "For the Lord himself will descend from heaven with a cry of command, with the voice of an archangel, and with the sound of the trumpet of God. And the dead in Christ will rise first. Then we who are alive, who are left, will be caught up together with them in the clouds to meet the Lord in the air, and so we will always be with the Lord" (4:16–17). This was Paul's pastoral message to a congregation of mostly young believers who were disheartened by death's forceful grip that claimed the lives of many among them and who were desperately trying to make sense of what it means to live as God's holy people in a world that is hostile to Christ. Paul expands their vision by placing them at the center of trinitarian action. He helps them to see how their part in a community of saints in an ongoing drama gives meaning to their present afflictions and gives them an eschatological hope worth fighting for. "Therefore encourage one another with these words" (4:18).

5

The Shape of a
Theodramatic Homiletic

I n the previous chapter we explored a dramatic model of theology. We saw how this model balances epic and lyric and grounds theology in the internal consistency of the biblical theodrama—a theodrama that gives a polyphonic witness to the Triune God, who renews all creation. Using the essential building blocks of dramatic theology, I have one goal in this chapter: to construct a *homiletical theology* that will animate sermons. I hope these sermons will be deeply committed to making known what Scripture says about God, who renews the world through Christ, while carefully considering what context the theodrama is performed in. What might preaching look like when seen through a theodramatic lens? What homiletical implications can we draw from dramatic theology? What convictions undergird a theodramatic approach to preaching? In this chapter we will explain the shape of a *theodramatic homiletic* by examining preaching's nature, purpose, and context.

The Nature of Theodramatic Preaching

Divine Proto-performance

Though discussed in the previous chapter, it's worth reiterating that the Bible is a script that discloses God's activities in history. However you understand the idea of *theodrama*—the drama of God; the drama that is performed by God; the drama in which God is the leading protagonist—the Bible is profoundly centered on actual actions of God in history. We can say that the Bible as a "textual record was *engendered by performance* 'in nature itself, in real space.'"[1] Scripture is thus "God's self-performance,"[2] or God's "self-communicative action."[3] The self-disclosing performance of God authorizes the biblical script. So the metaphor of the Bible as a script emphasizes the centrality of Scripture and God's story in preaching.

Of course the Bible as a script does more than chronicle God's self-communicative actions; it helps us see that human beings are at the center of the divine attention and action and that we are given important roles to play in it too. Yet it is paramount to the theodramatic homiletic to recognize that without the gift of God's self-performance, there is no action, no movement in time, and no script on which to base our own performance. As Balthasar says, "It is God who acts, on [humans], for [humans] and then together with [humans]; the involvement of [humans] in the divine action is *part of God's action, not a precondition of it.*"[4] The Bible is intended for enactment, but the initiative to do something lies not with the preacher or the congregation because it is God's performance that *elicits* the church's performance. In other words, God's words and actions are the *proto-performance*—"a source or impulse that gives rise to [other] performance[s]."[5] In the context of theater, proto-performance is "a prior performance, revived, revised, or reconstructed or simply used

1. Max Harris rephrases Karl Barth's idea of revelation. See Max Harris, *Theater and Incarnation* (Grand Rapids: Eerdmans, 1990), 50 (emphasis added). See also Karl Barth, *Church Dogmatics*, trans. G. W. Bromiley et al., 5 vols. (Edinburgh: T&T Clark, 1956–75), 1/1:115.

2. Charles Bartow, *God's Human Speech: A Practical Theology of Proclamation* (Grand Rapids: Eerdmans, 1997), 26.

3. Kevin Vanhoozer, "The Voice and the Actor: A Dramatic Proposal about the Ministry and Minstrelsy of Theology," in *Evangelical Futures: A Conversation on Theological Method*, ed. John G. Stackhouse (Grand Rapids: Baker Books, 2000), 74.

4. Hans Urs von Balthasar, *Theo-drama: Theological Dramatic Theory*, vol. 1, *Prolegomena* (San Francisco: Ignatius Press, 1989), 18 (emphasis added).

5. Richard Schechner, *Performance Studies: An Introduction*, 3rd ed. (New York: Routledge, 2013), 226. I'm using Richard Schechner's term *proto-performance* not only to designate God as the source of preaching performance but also to emphasize that divine words and actions are actual performances that give birth to human performance. Notice that any reference to divine performance in this section (unless indicated otherwise) connotes the collaborative work of the Triune God.

as a model or starting point for performance-to-be."[6] The Christian life, conversely, is not about revising or replicating what God has done but is instead a response to God's gracious initiative and revelation. Thus the Christian life contributes to the ongoing story with a fresh, contextualized performance of our own, modeled after God's. By God's Spirit we "continue the same action [that God has started] in new situations."[7] This does not suggest that God's actions are completed and done, as if preaching fills in and continues where God has left off in the story. The words "In the beginning, God" (Gen. 1:1) name God as the creator and originator of all things and also, by implication, the sustainer on which everything depends for continuation. So God—the Alpha and Omega—is the source of the church's performance, and he continues to carry out his will and plan and energizes the church for action. Paul speaks of this truth with confidence: "I am sure of this, that he who began a good work in you will bring it to completion at the day of Jesus Christ" (Phil. 1:6).

Preaching as Performance

Divine proto-performance gives rise not only to Christian performance in general but also, more specifically, to *preaching as performance.*[8] Preaching, in its essence, is a faithful response to God's preceding (and ongoing) actions. It is an expression—albeit small, frail, and imperfect—of reciprocity to God who "first loved us" (1 John 4:19) and "sent his Son to be the propitiation for our sins" (4:10). God's proto-performance of love is the source of the love we are called to show (perform for) our neighbors and, by loving them, to love God. Concerning the performative nature of preaching,

6. Schechner, *Performance Studies*, 226.

7. Kevin Vanhoozer, "A Drama-of-Redemption Model: Always Performing?," in *Four Views on Moving beyond the Bible to Theology*, ed. Gary T. Meadors (Grand Rapids: Zondervan, 2009), 174.

8. Relating preaching to performance is not so out of place in homiletical literature. Since the rise of the New Homiletic, there has been a surge of writing that investigates what is at the nexus of preaching and performance. Most of it draws from performance arts and applies the insights and principles gained to the art of preaching (e.g., sermon crafting, manuscript writing, memorization, delivery). Under the tutelage of these works, preachers and congregations alike have begun to mend the once-shattered link between the mind and body as they seek not only to comprehend the gospel but also to experience it. This section builds on current homiletical literature and also goes beyond past insights by envisioning preaching through the theological lens of theodrama.

Jana Childers writes, "'Christ as God's revelation is God's act; and our conveyance of Christ in preaching is Christ's act.' Sermons are act, active and action. They move or they ought to. They weave together—not just ideas but spirits. The essence of preaching is to be found in this action."[9]

In the performance of preaching "the sermon [is] transformed from something which is encoded in print on a page into an oral-aural event for both the preacher and hearer."[10] It is as if the "arrested performance"[11] of the biblical text comes alive and goes into full swing as words leap off the page to become transformative utterances that illumine souls, dismantle and reconstruct ideals, create epiphanies, evoke desires, and cause change in people and societies. The performance of preaching enables us to see beyond the words written across the pages of the Bible to what those words point to: the reality of the gospel made possible by real actions of God, which the church is invited to indwell. In the theatrical event of preaching, the written drama of Scripture comes alive by the Spirit through the preacher's embodiment for the gathered.

By defining preaching as performance here, we are, in a way, making Vanhoozer's theological vision more "dramatic" because he does not see preaching—or for that matter pastoral ministry—in terms of performance but as the work of *directing* that assists the church's enactment of the theodrama.[12] Although Vanhoozer points out that the pastor "is also a player in the drama who directs as much by example as by precept,"[13] he considers preaching a "penultimate performance,"[14] not performance itself. Yet we see no apparent need to demarcate what pastors do as actors and what they do in their ministries as directors. Likewise, no clear distinction in practice exists between when pastors direct by example

9. Jana Childers, *Performing the Word: Preaching as Theatre* (Nashville: Abingdon, 1998), 43. Childers quotes from P. T. Forsyth, *Positive Preaching and the Modern Mind* (Grand Rapids: Baker, 1980), 349.

10. Richard F. Ward, *Speaking from the Heart: Preaching with Passion* (Eugene, OR: Wipf & Stock, 2001), 77.

11. Beverly Whitaker Long and Mary Frances Hopkins, *Performing Literature: An Introduction to Oral Interpretation* (Englewood Cliffs, NJ: Prentice-Hall, 1982), 2.

12. See Kevin Vanhoozer, *The Drama of Doctrine: A Canonical Linguistic Approach to Christian Theology* (Louisville: Westminster John Knox, 2005), 447–49.

13. Vanhoozer, *Drama of Doctrine*, 448.

14. Vanhoozer sees preaching as "offering a direction for church performance, which means that it is dramaturgical utterance, a penultimate performance." Vanhoozer, email message to author, May 29, 2014.

versus by precept. It seems that pastors model faith for others to imitate through their own participation in God's drama. Among myriad ways that pastors model faith (since it can be argued that all ministry does that), their ministry through the Word and Sacrament is the most foundational. By helping people remember what God has done in Scripture, preaching draws out other performances, which continue in the same manner and spirit as God's actions and are guided and empowered by his Spirit. *The performance of preaching rises from God's proto-performance and induces other performances that reflect the Spirit's generative work in forming a holy people for God.* However, in the nature of performance, this is not just a unidirectional process. The church's performance also acts as a lens to inform, reassess, and adjust the performance of preaching to better interpret the canonical text authorized by God.

Linking the term *performance* with preaching can trigger anything from mild discomfort to strong rejection for many. A pejorative connotation that "to perform" from the pulpit means to feign a persona and act in a fictitious manner seems to make performance go against the very virtues and ethics of preaching. This perception extends beyond the pulpit and pertains to everyday life. So why should performance conjoin with preaching? Understanding preaching as performance expands the objective of *theological* reflection—reading and interpreting the Bible—from mere contemplation to the enactment of Scripture.[15] Richard Ward suggests that the repugnance of performance in preaching—and in theology—needs to be redeemed in light of the term's etymological basis. *Performance* is derived from the old French *par* + *fournir*, which means "to complete" or "to carry out thoroughly,"[16] and it can be paraphrased as "form coming through."[17] Just as music "fully exists only when brought to life in the

15. Richard Lischer reminds us that the goal of theology is not contemplation but preaching that embodies Scripture and brings it to life: "Preaching is the final expression of theology. It has been toward preaching that theology has been tending." Richard Lischer, *A Theology of Preaching: The Dynamic of the Gospel*, rev. ed. (Nashville: Abingdon, 1981), 27.

16. Ward, *Speaking from the Heart*, 77. See also Carol Simpson Stern and Bruce Henderson, *Performance: Texts and Contexts* (White Plains, NY: Longman, 1993), 546; Dwight Conquergood, "Communication as Performance: Dramaturgical Dimensions of Everyday Life," in *The Jensen Lectures: Contemporary Studies*, ed. John I. Sisco (Tampa: University of South Florida Press, 1982), 27.

17. Ward, *Speaking from the Heart*, 77. See Alla Bozarth-Campbell, *The Word's Body: An Incarnational Aesthetic of Interpretation* (Tuscaloosa: University of Alabama Press, 1979), 2.

world of sound,"[18] biblical interpretation and theology also consummate and fulfill their purpose through the performance of preaching. The importance of this point is underscored by theology's accountability to a proper hermeneutical practice of continuous reflection and reassessment of ideas and beliefs in light of praxis. Moreover, in light of the prevalent disintegration, stratification, and partiality of theological education to "theoretical" disciplines (e.g., biblical courses, systematic theology) over "practical" ones (e.g., preaching, evangelism), a performance orientation to theology renews commitment to Christian discipleship as an embodied practice that is embedded in one's actual context.

At the same time, understanding preaching as performance that is engendered by God's proto-performance recasts the purpose not only of theology but also of preaching. It does so in two constructive ways that address some of the pitfalls of the traditional and the conversational homiletics. First, it reinstitutes Christian formation as the *telos* of preaching.[19] Here, formation refers to shaping not only people's minds and hearts but also their actions. Genuine faith and transformation should always be expressed through right living. The sermon's end goal is neither to indoctrinate people with religious ideas nor to delight them by offering an electric spiritual experience. Balancing the epic and the lyric, preaching as a performance based on God's theodrama seeks to move people to performance by embracing and living out their new identities (or roles) as God's covenant people who join in God's reconciling work today.[20]

In chapter 1 we noted Augustine's threefold delineation of the purpose of preaching: teaching (*docere*), delighting (*delectare*), and moving (*movere*). We then discussed how, over time, the aspect of *teaching*, which was customary and most accentuated, became the trademark of the traditional homiletic.[21] In chapters 2 and 3 we saw that the conversational homiletic

18. Clayton J. Schmit, "What Comes Next? Performing Music and Proclaiming the Word," in *Performance in Preaching: Bringing the Sermon to Life*, ed. Jana Childers and Clayton J. Schmit (Grand Rapids: Baker Academic, 2008), 175.

19. We will explore this idea further in the next section.

20. Augustine, *De doctrina christiana*, trans. R. P. H. Green (Oxford: Clarendon, 1995), 4.12.74.

21. This, of course, is a broad observation based on the most prominent and enduring emphases in preaching throughout history. The preaching of various individuals (e.g., Bernard of Clairvaux, Catherine of Siena) and moments in church history (e.g., the medieval era, when poetic, artistic sermons thrived) show that sermons come in many forms, including those that

and, more generally, the New Homiletic represent a revived impulse for *delighting* listeners as preachers. In correspondence, homileticians shifted their interest to people's experience of texts and sermons as a Word-event that shapes the participants. The vision of preaching as a performance that generates other performances restores the third integral aspect of Augustine's definition: to *move* people to action by joining the Spirit's work in the world. Preaching galvanizes and stirs others to participate in the theodrama by conveying to listeners' minds and hearts a convincing, urgent enactment of the gospel that brings people face to face with God's glory.[22]

Second, preaching as performance recasts "all members of a speech community as potential artists, all utterances as potentially aesthetic, all events as potentially theatrical."[23] From a performance perspective, the congregation does not consist of passive listeners who merely receive a sermon. Rather, the church is a company of actors who share the work of interpreting and performing the theodrama. Preaching is the church's central and primary ministry as God's ordained method for proclaiming the good news (Rom. 10:14, 17; 2 Tim. 3:16–17; 4:2). However, a performance orientation to preaching recognizes the importance of other forms of the ministry of the Word. These other forms share in the task of edifying the church and making Christ known (e.g., Sunday school classes, small groups, the fellowship of believers).[24] Dependence on other

---

do not fall neatly into this categorization and incline more toward the mystical and lyrical. It is wise, therefore, to acknowledge the limitation of this generalization, especially because in a greater part of church history, cognitive or logical knowledge and experiential or affective knowledge were not separated as we in the post-Enlightenment era have construed them to be. Nonetheless, it is difficult to deny what has become the strongest and most lasting impression in preaching.

22. Jonathan Edwards notes that the manner in which God communicates to humankind is by allowing his glory to be "seen" and "rejoiced in" because "God is more glorified than if they only see it; his glory is then received by the soul, both by the understanding and by the heart" (Jonathan Edwards, The "Miscellanies," ed. Thomas Schafer, in *The Works of Jonathan Edwards* [New Haven: Yale University Press, 1994], 13:448). Shannon Craigo-Snell also shares this view and argues from a performance perspective informed by Don Saliers's theological ideas that Christian affections are "a kind of knowing that is not simply intellectual, but is also emotional and volitional. . . . Christian liturgy forms the person to know, feel, and will in ways that are shaped by the Christian story of salvation, known in Scripture." Shannon Craigo-Snell, *The Empty Church: Theater, Theology, and Bodily Hope* (New York: Oxford, 2014), 38, 39.

23. Ronald J. Pelias and James Van Oosting, "A Paradigm for Performance Studies," *Quarterly Journal of Speech* 73 (1987): 224.

24. Timothy Keller's broad ecclesial understanding of the ministry of the Word is helpful. He notes that there are at least three forms or levels to the ministry of the Word: (1) an

ministries does not diminish the role of preaching but elevates Christian discipleship as a task of utmost importance that the entire faith community must shoulder together. Indeed, it takes a village to raise a child of God. So the performance perspective celebrates the priesthood of all believers as having equal accessibility to God and the potential and shared responsibility to carry out God's mission. Seeing preaching in this light tears down an artificial compartmentalization of religious and secular actions, which breeds half-hearted dedication, and bares our lives entirely before God, whose holiness demands unreserved consecration.

Representing the Theodramatic Reality of Scripture

To be precise, preaching is not simply a performance of the gospel discourse per se but an evocation of *"the world/theodrama that the text/ script presupposes, entails, and implies."*[25] This means that the end goal in reading Scripture is not simply grasping "the author's intention [or] what an author says (the sense) but rather what the author is talking about (the referent)"[26]—*the nature of the gospel that has direct impact on our view of reality.* Preaching is, therefore, both discursive (i.e., it tells a story) and expository (i.e., it recovers the significance of the story).[27] On one level, preaching announces and gives an account of the biblical narrative (sense/discursive), but on a deeper level, it clarifies, explains, illustrates, and contextualizes for today's listeners the truth of new life in Christ (referent/expository). Accordingly, preaching is a performance that strives *to represent the theodramatic reality that Scripture denotes.*

---

informal Christian witness by teaching and admonishing one another, (2) a presentation of the Word in the forms of counseling, instructing, teaching, and evangelizing, and (3) preaching sermons in a public worshiping assembly. He says, "While we will always require a host of varied forms of Word ministry, the specific public ministry of preaching is irreplaceable. . . . A church's gospel ministry should be 'pulpit-centered, but not pulpit-restricted.' So there are three levels of Word ministry, and they are all crucial and support one another. The public preaching of Christ in the Christian assembly (level 3) is a unique way that God speaks to and builds up people, and it sets up the more organic forms of Word ministry at levels 1 and 2. Likewise, the skilled and faithful communication at levels 1 and 2 prepares people to be receptive to preaching." Tim Keller, *Preaching: Communicating Faith in an Age of Skepticism* (New York: Viking, 2015), 1–7.

25. Vanhoozer, "Drama-of-Redemption Model," 165.
26. Vanhoozer, "Drama-of-Redemption Model," 166.
27. Bartow, *God's Human Speech*, 104.

What does it mean for preaching to represent this reality? The mimetic nature of preaching shares similarities with the theater's nature to echo and image a script or an original performance. The goal of theater is to "transcend slavish representation [of script] and create a difference"[28] that renders meaning in fresh ways for the present audience. Likewise, in its engagement with Scripture, church traditions, audience, and the wider culture, preaching communicates *the theological meaning and significance of the theodrama*. As Joel Green asserts, to read the Bible as Scripture is to recognize that it records and interprets selective ordering of historical events based on their significance in order to shape a uniquely Christian worldview in light of God's renewing work through Christ.[29] Accordingly, the task of biblical interpretation and preaching is not merely a historical matter of reconstructing the past. While it is a cultural product shaped by the people and events of an ancient world, the Bible also transcends particularity and speaks to contemporary listeners, shaping their identity as those "not of the world" (John 15:19; 17:16) as it once did for the original hearers. Bookended by creation in Genesis and new creation in Revelation, the Bible portrays a drama about the past and future: despite humanity's sin and rebellion and "through many [present] dangers, toils, and snares" as exiles living in this world, we will one day share in God's glory as those redeemed by Christ and kept alive by the Spirit, who wills and empowers us to do good works.[30] Preaching provides hearers with this conceptual framework from the biblical drama in order to help us understand the existential state of our lives and how our performance befits the story.

Insofar as preaching is a *re*-enactment or *re*-presentation of the theodrama and God's prior actions described in Scripture, there is a *re-performative* quality to the ministry of the Word. That is to say, preaching does not merely describe and exposit the biblical story, but it is the very means by which God continues to show mercy and grace and accomplish salvation (Rom. 1:16; 10:17; 1 Cor. 1:21; Heb. 4:12–13). There is power

28. Here Sven Lütticken is referring to reenactment plays, but even in this type of performance art, the objective is not to image the original event but to re-present it for the present audience. See Sven Lütticken, *Life Once More: Forms of Reenactment in Contemporary Art* (Amsterdam: Witte de With, 2005), 5.

29. See Joel B. Green, *Practicing Theological Interpretation: Engaging Biblical Texts for Faith and Formation* (Grand Rapids: Baker Academic, 2011), 43–56.

30. Green, *Practicing Theological Interpretation*, 29–42.

in his Word (Ps. 19:7–11; 2 Tim. 3:16–17; 1 Pet. 1:23). A theological re-presentation of Scripture enables listeners to "hear in the words of Scrip-ture the word of God speaking in the present tense."[31] Here Green agrees with William Willimon's observation: "Barth will say that we can speak of God because God has spoken and God will speak again; therefore our preaching is bound to have a repetitive quality about it. *Preaching is always a reenactment of the primal miracle, 'And God said . . .'*"[32]

Frederick Buechner also relates a similar sentiment: "The fairy tale of the gospel [has] . . . one crucial difference from all other fairy tales, which is that the claim made for it is that it is true, that *it not only happened once upon a time but has kept on happening ever since and is happening still*. To preach the Gospel in its original power and mystery is to claim in whatever way the preacher finds it possible to claim that *once upon a time is this time, now*."[33] These words underscore the point that preach-ing as a re-presentation of God's performance goes beyond *recalling* what God has done and *refreshes* our awareness of God's ongoing action so the gospel becomes good news for today that makes us lean into God's future. Preaching is an outward and ordinary means through which God deals graciously with his people—namely, by extending his restoration and renewal to us. Preaching is divine encore performance, if we will—the divinely instituted means to extend God's re-creating, transformative min-istry in listeners. Thus, in theologically *re*-presenting Scripture, preaching enables the church to see the continuity of God's actions through time and to experience God's mercies as new every time we gather. God has never ceased working, and the drama depicted in the Bible is the same, uninterrupted drama that is unfolding even in our lives.

The story does not end there, however. God will keep carrying out his plan until the glorious resolution of a new heaven and a new earth. Between the past and future, we are faced with a choice: Do we believe this story to be true? How will we respond to what God has done for us? Will we join God and participate in a story that is bigger than our lives?

31. Green, *Practicing Theological Interpretation*, 5.
32. William H. Willimon, *Conversations with Barth on Preaching* (Nashville: Abingdon, 2006), 101 (emphasis added).
33. Frederick Buechner, *Telling the Truth: The Gospel as Tragedy, Comedy, and Fairytale* (New York: HarperOne, 1977), 90–91 (emphasis added).

The performance of preaching re-presents the *past* (i.e., the prior actions of God) to bear on the *present* and in so doing offers the present as a decisive moment for believers to fashion their *future.*[34] To put it differently, by re-presenting Scripture, preaching reminds the church of what God has already accomplished through Jesus and revisits judgments and promises being fulfilled and not yet fulfilled. Don Saliers refers to this function as that of worship in "remembering the future."[35] Remembering the past and future empowers the church to live the present in light of the theodramatic reality: both relishing what has been granted to us at this moment through Christ and the Spirit and vigilantly expecting what is guaranteed to us by Christ. Preaching as a communicative action is thus always "directed toward the 'already' and the 'not yet' of God's kingdom . . . of remembering and expecting."[36] In preaching, epic and lyric coalesce: as the church is caught up in the theodrama, it is able to fully experience the present moment (lyric) without losing sight of "where [it] is in the theodrama—in which scene and which act—and how [it] should respond"[37] (epic).

In all this, the performance of preaching should be seen not as a finished, final performance but as a rehearsal of the theodrama based on our ongoing interaction with Scripture, church tradition, the local and global witness of God's people today, and our contexts.[38] Since the church lives in the tension of God's kingdom that is already here and not yet fully realized, all Christian performance in the present—including preaching—is flawed, limited, and transient. For this reason, preaching may be understood as an "ongoing rehearsal of our faith, [a constant reinterpretation of] the Scriptures in our lives as a part of the community of faith to which we belong."[39]

34. Similarly, Casey Barton observes the biblical drama's "anachronistic" ability to fuse the horizons of past, present, and future. In preaching, the present moment of the church's gathering and the past or the future moment of the biblical drama intersect and open up space that allows for participation from worshipers. See Casey Clarence Barton, *Preaching through Time: Anachronism as a Way Forward for Preaching* (Eugene, OR: Cascade, 2017).
35. Don E. Saliers, *Worship as Theology: A Foretaste of Glory Divine* (Nashville: Abingdon, 1994), 217.
36. Gerben Heitink, *Practical Theology: History, Theory, Action Domains; Manual for Practical Theology*, trans. Reinder Bruinsma (Grand Rapids: Eerdmans, 1999), 155.
37. Vanhoozer, "Drama-of-Redemption Model," 170.
38. As will be further explored in this chapter, preaching is not shaped by the pastor alone but by the congregation's shared stories, memories, interactions, and conversations.
39. Todd E. Johnson and Dale Savidge, *Performing the Sacred: Theology and Theatre in Dialogue* (Grand Rapids: Baker Academic, 2009), 94. See also Shannon Craigo-Snell, "Command

Christian formation is neither instantaneous nor a onetime event. The formation of character and the embodiment in action take place in an ongoing dynamic relationship, as do rehearsal and performance. Through repeated rehearsal and performance, our *being* and *action* become integrated so we *grow into* what we enact. Balthasar explains it this way: "Only the action itself will reveal who each individual is; and it will not reveal, through successive unveilings, primarily who the individual *always was*, but rather who [one] *is to become* through the action, through [one's] encounter with others and through the decision [the person] makes. There is at least a reciprocal relationship between the 'was' and the 'will be.'"[40]

The rehearsal of preaching enacts what is true about *who we are today*, but it also helps us realize *who we can be in Christ* through the Spirit's ministry. We come "just as we are" to the moment of preaching and worship, but we also practice "ideals" of who we are called to be as we turn our eyes to Jesus.[41]

To recapitulate: in the event of preaching, the church does more than "remember the past acts of God's interventions in human history; [its members] rehearse and encounter the events as present realities."[42] At the same time, the church anticipates the eschatological future when the rehearsal ends and pure worship in God's presence begins. Until that day, the church is "invited to participate in the drama [of God], imitating in their corporate life and in their worship, 'both public and private,' the 'true' heavenly temple and the pioneer entry of Christ into heaven on their behalf."[43] As Paul states in Ephesians 4:13, "God's goal is for us to become mature adults—to be fully grown, measured by the standard of the fullness of Christ" (CEB). Preaching is "restored behavior"[44] that strives to re-present God's prior performance to the church so that we may "grow up in every way into him who is the head, into Christ" (Eph.

Performance: Rethinking Performance Interpretation in the Context of *Divine Discourse*," *Modern Theology* 16, no. 4 (2000): 475–94.

40. Hans Urs von Balthasar, *Theo-Drama: Theological Dramatic Theory*, vol. 2, *Dramatis Personae: Man in God* (San Francisco: Ignatius Press, 1990), 11.

41. See Shannon Craigo-Snell, *The Empty Church: Theater, Theology, and Bodily Hope* (Oxford: Oxford University Press, 2014), 19.

42. Johnson and Savidge, *Performing the Sacred*, 134.

43. Harris, *Theater and Incarnation*, 53.

44. Richard Schechner, *Performance Studies: An Introduction*, 3rd ed. (New York: Routledge, 2013), 22.

4:15). Preaching as performance "is never for the first time" and should "always [be] subject to revision."[45] As contexts and historical circumstances change, the preacher (along with the congregation) repeats and rehearses the theodrama in both personal and corporate life to better enact it until our worship is made perfect in God's presence.

The Purpose of Theodramatic Preaching

Moving the Church to Participate in the Reality of "Being in Christ"

Preaching as a theological performance of the gospel reality shows the continuity of God's actions in Scripture and his actions today toward the denouement of his salvation drama. As discussed previously, preaching's purpose can be described with the Augustinian idea of *moving* people to participate in the theodrama through the preacher's own performance of preaching. Leonora Tubbs Tisdale expresses a similar idea when she compares the preacher to a folk dancer whose performance elicits the participation of others:

> Often we speak of preaching as if it were a performance—akin to a ballet—in which the goal is for everyone in the audience to go away marveling over the skill of the lead performer, the preacher. But when preaching is viewed as folk dance, the goal is quite different: namely, that the leader *models* the dance of faith in such an accessible, imaginative, earthy, and encouraging way that everyone—young and old, visitor and member, old timer and newcomer—*will want to put on his or her own dancing shoes and join in.*[46]

So preaching impresses the vision of the theodrama on the hearts and minds of the congregation and stirs them to take on their role as Christian disciples too. The performance of preaching therefore has a contagious effect: "It is an act whose purpose it is to kick off the chain and effect, to tip the end domino, to *set motion in motion.*"[47]

45. Richard Schechner, *Between Theater and Anthropology* (Philadelphia: University of Pennsylvania Press, 1985), 37.
46. Leonora Tubbs Tisdale, *Preaching as Local Theology and Folk Art* (Minneapolis: Fortress, 1997), 125–26 (emphasis added).
47. Jana Childers, "Seeing Jesus: Preaching as Incarnational Act," in *Purposes of Preaching*, ed. Jana Childers (St. Louis: Chalice, 2004), 44 (emphasis added).

The concept of *modeling* faith to encourage faith in others should not be foreign to those who are familiar with the epistles.[48] These writings repeatedly instruct readers to imitate (*mimēsis*) other mature Christians who practice their faith in Jesus Christ (1 Cor. 4:16; 11:1; Phil. 3:17; 2 Thess. 3:7–9; 1 Tim. 4:12, 15–16; 2 Tim. 3:10–11; Titus 2:7; Heb. 13:7). For example, Paul encourages Titus, a fellow minister to "show [him]self in all respects to be a *model* of good works" (Titus 2:7). The charge to Titus resembles Peter's exhortation to the elders of the churches in Asia Minor: to "not [be] domineering over those in [their] charge, but [be] *examples* to the flock" (1 Pet. 5:3). In these passages, Paul and Peter are not urging believers to mimic *them* as the final cause of faith but, ultimately, to imitate *Jesus*, after whom the apostles model themselves. Hence modeling faith stirs and inspires people to act as "little Christs" who resemble their true Teacher and Lord.[49] Acting as Christ's disciples in the theodrama involves more than going through pious motions; instead, we fully assume our new identity and character by having "the mind of Christ" (1 Cor. 2:16) at all times so that our attitude, disposition, thoughts, desires, and behaviors are shaped by it.[50] Preaching's role, then, is "to train and discipline the believer's mind, heart, and imagination to think, desire, see—and then *do*—reality as it is in Jesus Christ."[51] The idea of "seeing" and then "doing" does not suggest a separation between interpretation and performance or relegate rehearsal and embodiment of beliefs to a secondary place. Neither does it mean that interpretation and performance are unidirectional, onetime events. We see and then do reality in Christ in the sense that theological interpretation and performance begin by beholding what God has done in Jesus Christ on our behalf. The reality that our understanding develops and deepens with each performance and that our performance itself is a profoundly interpretive act cannot be overemphasized, any more than we could overemphasize that theological endeavor

---

48. Vanhoozer also explores the concept of *mimēsis* (imitation), but his interest is more expressly on how disciples are to imitate Christ. See Kevin J. Vanhoozer, *Faith Speaking Understanding: Performing the Drama of Doctrine* (Louisville: Westminster John Knox, 2014), 123–25. My argument here is broader than Vanhoozer's claim because I am saying that Spirit-empowered preaching is a means of grace that can stir people's desire and godly imagination to imitate Christ.

49. See Vanhoozer, *Faith Speaking Understanding*, 157.

50. Vanhoozer, *Faith Speaking Understanding*, 188–89.

51. Vanhoozer, "Drama-of-Redemption Model," 170 (emphasis original).

begins with regarding God's glory revealed in Christ. God sought us out and made a claim on our lives. This action is where theological reflection and our response start. So the ministry of preaching builds up the church by making it more fully aware of its identity in Christ and moves it to live out this reality to the fullest extent.

To properly understand the notion of preaching as a performance that models faith, we need to set this discussion in a broader context that considers the role of the congregation. Vanhoozer believes that "every member of the church plays an important role"[52] and that the congregation participates in the interactive theater of the gospel by "making the appropriate response . . . of belief and the obedient faith."[53] Beyond this, however, the congregation remains more or less passive recipients of biblical interpretation for Vanhoozer. Yet aligning his theological ideas more with the view of theology as "a theory of action"[54] and of the theater as a thoroughly communal undertaking expands and reenvisions the congregation's role as active contributors to biblical interpretation and to the performance of the church's mission to the world. Theology that stems from a critical interaction between theory and praxis takes the congregation's experience seriously as an essential object of reflection. If we believe that the missionary God actively prepares, equips, and sends the church into the world, where he is already at work through the Spirit, the members of the congregation are important witnesses to God-in-action in the world, witnesses who bring their potent observations and insights to contribute to our understanding of the theodrama.[55] Bruce Ellis Benson notes that the Holy Spirit "*continues* to speak in new ways as the Word goes forth in the world," just as "God can speak in new ways through canon formation."[56]

52. Vanhoozer, *Drama of Doctrine*, 414.
53. Vanhoozer, *Faith Speaking Understanding*, 35.
54. Theology as "a theory of action" rises from the praxis to inform theory. See Heitink, *Practical Theology*, 124–32.
55. See Craig Van Gelder, *The Ministry of the Missional Church* (Grand Rapids: Baker Books, 2007); Ray S. Anderson, *The Soul of Ministry: Forming Leaders for God's People* (Louisville: Westminster John Knox, 1997); Mark Lau Branson and Juan F. Martínez, *Churches, Cultures, and Leadership: A Practical Theology of Congregations and Ethnicities* (Downers Grove, IL: InterVarsity Press, 2011); Alan J. Roxburgh, *Missional Map-Making: Skills for Leading in Times of Transition* (San Francisco: Jossey-Bass, 2010).
56. Bruce Ellis Benson, "Improvising Text, Improvising Communities," in *Resonant Witness: Conversations between Music and Theology*, ed. Jeremy Begbie and Steven Guthrie (Grand Rapids: Eerdmans, 2011), 303 (emphasis original).

If this is the case, even from the viewpoint of theater arts, it behooves preachers to see the congregation as fellow actors who "bring the latent meaning in the text to life in ways relevant to the community at large."[57] A crucial aspect of what actors do is to imagine in collaboration with the director how the script may be embodied in a particular context. "Actors, directors, producers, set designers, and so on are all part of the process of interpretation,"[58] which unfolds continuously in the ongoing rehearsal of the play. Likewise, the church as a theater discerns together how the biblical script can be best enacted in every circumstance. For this reason, the sermon is, and should always be, every bit the congregation's expression of faith and testimony about God who is at work in their lives. Emerging from a lively interaction with Scripture, Christian tradition, liturgy, congregation, and the world, the sermon should represent the theodramatic reality for all to savor. Thus the sermon not only "proclaims 'to' but also 'out of the midst of' and 'on behalf of' a local faith community."[59] Although the minister takes the lead in modeling faith in the event of preaching, the entire church is called to "encourage one another and build one another up" (1 Thess. 5:11) and "consider how to stir up one another to love and good works" (Heb. 10:24). We are audiences to one another's faith performances. How we carry ourselves daily—positively or negatively—affects those within the Christian community and those outside.[60]

Deviating from performance terms for a moment, a musical analogy first used by Dietrich Bonhoeffer and later taken up by Jeremy Begbie may clarify the relationship between the biblical theodrama and the diversity of ecclesial reflections and experiences. Few things are thought of as more incompatible and contentious than love for God and love for good things in the world. Bonhoeffer not only brings these two contrasting concepts together but also orders them using the metaphor of *cantus firmus* and polyphony to show how one can flourish because of the other. In music, the *cantus firmus*, the preexisting thematic melody, both guards against the discord and chaos that can ensue when individual melodies take over

57. Johnson and Savidge, *Performing the Sacred*, 93.
58. Johnson and Savidge, *Performing the Sacred*, 93.
59. Tisdale, *Preaching as Local Theology and Folk Art*, 41.
60. Wesley Vander Lugt offers a thoughtful discussion on who constitutes the audience of the theodrama. See *Living Theodrama: Reimagining Theological Ethics* (Burlington, VT: Ashgate, 2014), 161–77.

and also harmonizes contrapuntal melodies to achieve fullness in sound through their interdependence. Applying this concept to theology, Bonhoeffer uses the expression "polyphony of life" to refer to earthly joys and affection, and he points to the *cantus firmus* of love of God, the giver of these good gifts, that enables the counterpoints of earthly love to flourish.[61] Jeremy Begbie adopts Bonhoeffer's idea when he refers to the "Pentecostal polyphony" of Christian identity, in which Christ is the *cantus firmus* and the church constitutes the polyphonic melodies around him. The church—as ones invited to the polyphony of the Trinity—is also a "polyphonic people" who display diversity within unity. In "Pentecostal polyphony . . . both the suffocating individualism of modernism and the erasure of personal uniqueness of postmodernism are overcome . . . [and our] identit[ies are] discovered not despite but above all *in and through* relationships of this kind."[62]

Returning to our discussion, the theodrama (i.e., the gospel) may also be thought of as the *cantus firmus* that grounds and fosters the polyphony of the church's interpretive performances. The *cantus firmus* of the biblical theodrama does not impede the church's performance but informs and anchors it even in turbulent, changing contexts. Bonhoeffer's reflection on the *cantus firmus* of Christ and the polyphony of life applies to preaching as well: "I want to tell you to have a good, clear, *cantus firmus*; that is the only way to a full and perfect sound, when the counterpoint has a firm support and can't come adrift or get out of tune, while remaining a distinct whole in its own right. Only a polyphony of this kind can give life a wholeness and at the same time assure us that nothing calamitous can happen as long as the *cantus firmus* is kept going. . . . Rely on the *cantus firmus*."[63]

When the *cantus firmus* of the theodrama resounds clearly, the counterpoints of diverse interpretations also flourish.

Reorienting a View of Reality

In one of the most well-known passages of the Bible, Paul instructs early Christians in Rome to "present your bodies as a living sacrifice, holy

61. Dietrich Bonhoeffer, *Letters and Papers from Prison* (London: SCM, 1972), 394.
62. See Jeremy Begbie, *Resounding Truth: Christian Wisdom in the World of Music* (Grand Rapids: Baker Academic, 2007), 270 (emphasis original).
63. Bonhoeffer, *Letters and Papers from Prison*, 303.

and acceptable to God" (Rom. 12:1). This presenting ourselves is not lip service or playacting; our "spiritual," "reasonable," or "true" worship that responds appropriately to God's unfathomable mercies constitutes an ongoing performance that consumes our whole being—where our bodies are the very sacrifice offered up in worship. To offer ourselves up to God in this way, Paul commands us: "Do not be conformed to this world, but be transformed by the renewal of your mind" (12:2), which to a significant degree serves as a measure for understanding how believers should act to please God. According to Paul, our new life through the Spirit offers a different way of thinking and being conscious of the world. The Spirit redefines and reorders reality so that we can relate to one another and to the world in light of the truth of the gospel.

Something similar can be said about preaching. In service of the Holy Spirit's ministry, preaching redefines and reorients people's view of reality. We are inundated and shaped by worldly discourses that tell us who we are and how we should think and live. Thousands of images, taglines, stories, and texts "preach" to us daily about human worth, happiness, success, and love. Preaching protests and breaks through these godless narratives and helps us see beyond them to "the things that are unseen. For the things that are seen are transient, but the things that are unseen are eternal" (2 Cor. 4:18). If faith is "the enduring ability to imagine life in a certain way,"[64] then preaching helps us "surrender . . . one set of images and [accept] . . . another."[65] Preaching reminds the church that we are a holy people called out of the world and baptized into God's grand drama that is about reconciling all things to Christ.

The Old Testament prophets did this too. At times the prophets shattered people's worldviews and false sense of religiosity and hope by exposing their sins, folly, injustice, spiritual nakedness, and poverty, even though people were flourishing outwardly. At other times the prophets altered people's sense of reality by helping them see God's nearness and love, not God's absence, indifference, or impotence—even in times of suffering.

The biblical drama overflows with examples of such reorientation. One great example is captured in the shocking opening words of Isaiah

---

64. Barbara Brown Taylor quotes James D. Whitehead from "The Religious Imagination," *Liturgy* 5 (1985): 54–59. See Barbara Brown Taylor, *The Preaching Life* (Chicago: Cowley, 1993), 44.
65. Taylor, *Preaching Life*, 44.

6:1: "In the year that King Uzziah died I saw the Lord sitting upon a throne, high and lifted up; and the train of his robe filled the temple." When the beloved King Uzziah died, marking the end of a long, prosperous era in Judah, reality looked bleak and tragic, especially with Assyria looming as a threat. Security was pulled out from underneath them. Hope had vanished. The future was swallowed up by death. But God opened Isaiah's eyes to see a vision of the state of things as they really are: a vision of the Lord who sits on a throne, high and exalted. The truth of the matter is that the only true, good King of Israel is still alive and sovereign, and he governs all affairs of the world with flawless justice and boundless love. Just as the seraphim call out to one another in pure delight and testify to one another about God's perfection, Isaiah and Judah are invited to see the reality that God's holiness radically reorients everything: their sense of self ("Woe is me!" v. 5), their view of the communities they are part of ("I dwell in the midst of a people with unclean lips," v. 5), and their understanding of the present and future as God sees, wills, and carries out his plans (God's love and redemption through judgment for his people). A vision of God and his faithful presence opens up to Isaiah a different world—not a world full of despair and ruin but "the whole earth [that] is full of [God's] glory" (v. 3). This vision gives a sense of purpose and direction for Isaiah. People need an external word from God to be cast and recast as God's holy people in his great story.

This kind of preaching is needed in a world that suffers from a "failure of imagination"[66]—the lack of ability to imagine the world in light of the good news of who God is. At a personal level our failed imaginations debilitate us from living to the fullest extent who we were created to be, and we instead choose to live by the ephemeral discourses of the world, chasing after small dreams that have no eternal significance.[67] At a larger level our "inability to be gripped by a vision of a world of justice" under God's kingdom manifests itself in the societies and cultures we have created that settle for less than God's intended *shalom*. Against this backdrop, preaching that represents the theodrama seeks to reinvigorate

---

66. Mark Labberton, *The Dangerous Act of Worship: Living God's Call to Justice* (Downers Grove, IL: InterVarsity Press, 2007), 148.
67. Labberton, *Dangerous Act of Worship*, 148.

languid imaginations by awakening and energizing believers to see, dream, and live out the reality of God's kingdom. Mark Labberton asserts that worship is "one of God's primary antidotes to our small-minded, human-bounded lives" that helps cultivate "a life that feeds from and imitates the imagination of God."[68]

Stated differently, the theatricality of preaching and worship opens up imaginative space mediated by Scripture for people to visualize and experience a different way of being in the world. This imaginative space allows us to inhabit theodramatic reality and to think and feel not as we have been conditioned by the world to do but as characters we are called to enact. Walter Brueggemann's words are helpful: "The biblical text . . . is an offer of an alternative script, and preaching this text is to explore *how the world is, if it is imagined through this alternative script. . . .* The work of preaching is an act of imagination, that is, an offer of an image through which perception, experience, and finally faith can be reorganized in alternative ways."[69] The world operates from "the long established 'givens'" that "prevail because they are accepted beyond criticism," and "they will prevail until a counter-'as' is imagined and voiced."[70] Preaching overturns these treasured claims and frees our imagination from captivity to those things by offering a "counterimagination"[71] that renders reality in light of the gospel. The Spirit uses the preacher's words and actions to breathe new life into worn-out imaginations so that we can begin to "see the world, each other, and ourselves as God sees us, and to live as if God's reality were the only one that mattered."[72]

Recognizing divine presence in the world is no easy task. As Buechner describes it, "The tragedy of the human condition" is living "in a world where again and again God is not present, at least not in the way and to the degree that [humanity] needs him."[73] But we may describe faith, at least in part, as an ability to recognize God's presence and the way his

68. Labberton, *Dangerous Act of Worship*, 148.

69. Walter Brueggemann, *Cadences of Home: Preaching among Exiles* (Louisville: Westminster John Knox, 1997), 30, 32 (emphasis added).

70. Walter Brueggemann, *Texts under Negotiation: The Bible and Postmodern Imagination* (Minneapolis: Fortress, 1993), 15.

71. Brueggemann, *Texts under Negotiation*, 20.

72. Taylor, *Preaching Life*, 44.

73. Buechner, *Telling the Truth*, 53.

kingdom is engulfing us.[74] Thus the role of preaching, however partially, is to demonstrate and incite faith through theological interpretation that frames people's worldview. Preaching is an exercise in "interpretive leadership"[75] or "spiritual interpretation"[76] that models the faith to be attentive to and recognize the in-breaking kingdom of God in the world. Pastors offer a theological interpretation of the world to shape a community of interpreters "that learn how to deal with texts [of various kinds, inscribed and experiential] in such a way that they participate more fully in God's initiatives."[77]

Various practical theological approaches exist to tackle such a task, but Thomas Groome's "shared praxis approach" to education in Christian faith serves as one example that involves the congregation as agent-subjects in the reflection-action process.[78] This is not the only way to engage the congregation and train their imaginations for God's presence. Nonetheless, this model helpfully illustrates how preaching can do that work. As a quick overview, Groome's practical-theological method begins with a focusing activity and has five subsequent movements. The aim of the focusing activity is to turn the community's gaze toward a common theme in the present praxis—such as their interests, experiences, questions, or beliefs—that generates interest and unity and has the potential for a lively engagement in the movements to follow. In a sermon, this may take the

74. A. W. Tozer puts it this way: "A spiritual kingdom lies all about us, enclosing us, embracing us, altogether within reach of our inner selves, waiting for us to recognize it. God Himself is here waiting for our response to His presence. This eternal world will come alive to us the moment we begin to reckon upon its reality." See A. W. Tozer, *The Pursuit of God: The Human Thirst for the Divine* (Camp Hill, PA: WingSpread, 2006), 50.

75. See Mark Lau Branson, "Ecclesiology and Leadership for the Missional Church," in *The Missional Church in Context: Helping Congregations Develop Contextual Ministry*, ed. Craig Van Gelder (Grand Rapids: Eerdmans, 2007), 118–25. See also Branson and Martínez, *Churches, Cultures, and Leadership*, 210–31.

76. D. Scott Cormode, *Making Spiritual Sense: Christian Leaders as Spiritual Interpreters* (Eugene, OR: Wipf & Stock, 2006).

77. Branson, "Ecclesiology and Leadership for the Missional Church," 118–19. On a similar point, Thomas Long observes that the church no longer exists in a Christian land, as a vast number of today's hearers have "lost their grip on the gospel story and are struggling to form a coherent Christian life" (*Preaching from Memory to Hope* [Louisville: Westminster John Knox, 2009], 17). In such an era, when "making ethical sense of things for themselves may well be precisely what [hearers] cannot do, or are reluctant to do," preachers must act as "moral guides" who *"model in the sermon itself the internal processing of narratives that a previous generation of preachers could entrust fully to the hearers"* (15, emphasis added).

78. In the following section, examples provided in parentheses are my own.

form of an introduction that connects with the congregation's concerns, questions, and joys or pertains to shared culture (e.g., national tragedy, local news, pop culture events).

Movement 1 follows by inviting participants to "name or express an aspect of their own and/or their society's present praxis"[79] that ties in with the theme raised in the focusing activity. Here the purpose is to encourage participants to be honest and attentive to who they are as beings in a particular time and place. Groome encourages preachers to use thought-provoking questions that help people intentionally reflect on the present moment (e.g., What image comes to your mind when you think of happiness?), or, alternatively, preachers could name latent emotions and assumptions that may bring up deeper personal awareness (e.g., We all desire true happiness in life, and we're willing to do so much for it).

Movement 2 takes what Movement 1 began (i.e., recognition of the present praxis) and drives it further by encouraging *critical* reflection on the present action by analyzing its personal and social reasons (e.g., assumptions, prejudices, ideologies), sociocultural memory (e.g., sociohistorical and biographical sources of present praxis), and imagination for a preferred future (e.g., consequences of present praxis and possible ways forward that pertain to individuals and community). This movement allows participants to understand and assess their own stories or visions in relation to the generative theme shared at the beginning. Preachers in this movement can also raise questions that guide deep, honest reflection (e.g., Where do your ideas of happiness come from?) or offer suggestive analysis of the praxis using tools of philosophy, history, and social sciences that encourage critical consideration (e.g., Perhaps some of us base our understanding of happiness on what our culture recognizes and celebrates).

Movement 3 makes a Christian story accessible to participants (i.e., "symbolizes the faith life of the Christian community over history and in the present, as expressed through Scripture, traditions, liturgies and so forth"). It also makes a Christian vision accessible (i.e., "reflects the promises and demands that arise from the Story to empower and mandate Christians to live now for the coming of God's reign for all creation").[80]

---

79. Thomas H. Groome, *Sharing Faith: A Comprehensive Approach to Religious Education and Pastoral Ministry* (Eugene, OR: Wipf & Stock, 1991), 175.

80. Groome, *Sharing Faith*, 215.

Building on Movements 1 and 2, the purpose of this process is to foster a genuine interaction between the Christian story or vision and participants' stories or visions. The sermon should examine the world *of*, *behind*, and *before* the text so that the congregation hears what the text is saying— what it might have meant to the first hearers, what wisdom it holds for the present context, and what response it invites from them (e.g., if Psalm 1 was the sermon text, the preacher would explore the text's exegetical, literary, historical, and theological significance in relation to the theme of true "happiness" or "blessedness" in living according to God's covenantal instructions and directions).

The work in Movement 4 provides space to imagine a way forward for the participants by critically appropriating the Christian story or vision to their lives. By "appropriation" here, Groome means that "participants integrate Christian Story/Vision by personal agency into their own identity and understanding, that they make it their own, judge and come to see for themselves how their lives are to be shaped by it and how they are to be reshapers of its historical realization in their place and time."[81] Preachers can "model a dialectic appropriation of the exegesis and invite participants to do likewise" or raise questions that invite reflection for the same purpose.[82] For example, we may note in the sermon that living by God's covenantal "script" may appear foolish to the world, but Psalm 1 teaches that this is wisdom for living a truly blessed life. We may ask our listeners, What script are you following today? What areas of your life need to be (further) reoriented, starting today, to live according to God's script? And if we are striving to abide in God, maybe some of us also need to remember the promise and hope conveyed in the image of a fruitful tree.

Movement 5 works in tandem with Movement 4 to invite participants to discern the appropriate response to the sermon and make explicit decisions to live out their faith in the world. Decisions may vary as cognitive, affective, and behavioral, and they may pertain to personal, interpersonal, or sociopolitical levels, but the bottom line is to give participants an opportunity to digest what they heard in the sermon and begin shaping a new way forward in their praxis, following the Spirit's lead. Groome cautions

81. Groome, *Sharing Faith*, 250.
82. Groome, *Sharing Faith*, 378.

against defaulting to "moralizing exhortations" in this process that take away the congregation's agency, and he instead encourages preachers to pose questions that foster further reflection or name possible implications for an embodied experiment (e.g., How might our words and actions be different if we begin and end our days by turning to God's Word?). The reflection-action process does not end with the sermon but continues in the personal, interpersonal, and communal life of the congregation's members. As reflections, experiences, and experimentations on faith shape the life pattern of the church, formation happens in the nexus of contemplation and action.

Forming Christian Performers

It is not enough for the church to merely see the world in light of the gospel, but as discussed so far, God's people must live as though the claims of the gospel are true. This is not referring to simple application as a linear, one-step move that translates biblical concepts, ideas, and principles and puts them into operation. The work of ongoing, critical reflection on the biblical script (through rehearsal and in conversation with other players, ecclesial heritage, and context) is messy, interactive, experimental, and multidimensional. This is because formation and performance are intertwined processes that feed off each other. Through the continuous cycle of praxis-theory-praxis, preaching seeks to form Christian performers who can faithfully and creatively enact their roles as ones in Christ in changing contexts.

As we might imagine, skillful acting consists of more than the ability to recite lines with precision and carry out routine actions like programmed robots. A well-trained actor can proactively engage the complexity of the play with gracefulness, flexibility, and disciplined creativity in interaction with others and the environment in order to advance the story. Such competence develops over time through a rhythm of reflection and practice that cultivates habits that become part of one's character. For this reason, among others, improvisation provides a fruitful metaphor for Christian performance.[83]

---

83. A sampling of works that explore improvisation as a metaphor for Christian living includes Vanhoozer, *Drama of Doctrine*; Samuel Wells, *Improvisation: The Drama of Christian*

Improvisation, in the context of our discussion, is the ability to embody the gospel reality in every unpredictable situation in life in a way that honors the biblical script and is rooted in the church's historical witness. This represents an ongoing engagement with other players and praxis. Simply put, the ability to stay in our characters as "little Christs" who see and subsist in the theodramatic reality at all times is learning to improvise with the biblical script.[84] Although improvisation may look spontaneous, it is actually a well-rehearsed action that results from an imagination nurtured and disciplined over time by the script, the church's performance tradition, and the collaborative work of the actors. Following Christ and becoming like him require disciplined practice and a regimen characterized by constant dying to sin and living in righteousness (1 Pet. 2:24). It is the hard work that involves surrendering old habits and putting on new ones that allow us to skillfully and wisely live in the world as little Christs. Forming "right" habits is paramount because familiar, rehearsed actions eventually become "second nature."[85] Vanhoozer describes "genuine improvisation" as "a matter of *freedom* and *fittingness*. Disciples improvise each time they exercise Christian freedom fittingly, in obedient response to the gracious word of God that set it in motion. Improvising to the glory of God is ultimately a matter simply of being who one has been created to be in Christ, so that one responds freely and fittingly as if by reflex or second nature."[86]

In order to stay in character and improvise the biblical script in new circumstances, believers need to develop three hermeneutical senses: canonical, catholic, and contextual. Developing the canonical sense has to do with "acquiring biblical, literary, and canonical competence," which enables disciples to "understand the overall story line of the Scriptures and especially the nature and role of the church." The catholic sense

---

Ethics (Grand Rapids: Brazos, 2004); Stanley Hauerwas, *The Peaceable Kingdom: A Primer in Christian Ethics* (London: SCM, 1984); and Vander Lugt, *Living Theodrama*.

84. Vanhoozer, *Drama of Doctrine*, 128–29. See also Wells, *Improvisation*, 65.

85. Wells, *Improvisation*, 75. Will Durant quotes Aristotle's *Nicomachean Ethics* (2.4) in this famous quote: "Excellence is an art won by training and habituation: we do not act rightly because we have virtue or excellence, but we rather have these because we have acted rightly; 'these virtues are formed in man by his doing the actions'; we are what we repeatedly do. Excellence, then, is not an act but a habit." Will Durant, *The Story of Philosophy: The Lives and Opinions of the Greater Philosophers* (New York: Pocket Books, 2006), 98.

86. Vanhoozer, *Faith Speaking Understanding*, 191 (emphasis added).

relates to the previous performances of God's people in Scripture and in church tradition that enable disciples to "learn the deep patterns of biblical judgment about how to speak and act so as to continue the same story of Christ in different contexts." The cultivation of the contextual sense involves learning to grapple with "the conceptual resources at hand" and "appropriating them for gospel purposes."[87] These three senses equip believers to be skillful improvisers who—as guided by the Scriptures, the tradition of the church, and appropriateness to the context—have the ability to contribute to an ongoing story of God's actions in the world. Preaching serves to develop these senses in believers so that Christian disciples can live as ones whose minds and hearts are *engraved* with the divine law (i.e., have the mind of Christ) and so are free to improvise as God's people in every situation (Heb. 8:10).

The Context of Theodramatic Preaching

The Covenantal Context of Preaching

The ministry of preaching involves God, the preacher, and the congregation. It is an activity that concerns God and his people. Accordingly, the term that best describes the context of preaching is *covenant*. It is important to locate our discussion about the performance of preaching in this context because without the covenantal backdrop, preaching can be reduced simply to a language event. At a minimum, treating the sermon strictly as a speech-act leads to the misguided thinking that preaching as a performative utterance can be "happy" as long as it meets the necessary conditions of being "conventional, suitable, correct, complete, and sincere."[88] Yet the faultiness of such a syllogism becomes apparent when held up to most preachers' experiences: even sermons that fall short of meeting the criteria of a happy performance can flourish against all odds when God chooses to use them for his purposes. And sermons meeting these criteria may have no effect on the life of the congregation. It fol-

---

87. Vanhoozer, *Faith Speaking Understanding*, 205.

88. John Rottman cautions against the danger of curtailing a discussion on preaching performance to a discourse on language event. See John M. Rottman, "Performative Language and the Limits of Performance in Language," in *Performance in Preaching: Bringing the Sermon to Life*, ed. Jana Childers and Clayton J. Schmit (Grand Rapids: Baker Academic, 2008), 67–86.

lows, then, that preaching cannot be reduced to a language event because doing so impinges on divine freedom and strips the pulpit of its mystery. Furthermore, if we see preaching simply in terms of a speech-act, we dismiss the transcendent aspect of performance that exists "between the words, in the tiny spaces between the words."[89] In other words, something happens in preaching that we cannot explain through philosophy or analysis.

Only theology supplies the right frame from which to understand the mysteries and marvels of preaching that resist philosophical explanation. That frame is the covenant. The covenant depicts the haunting scandal of a holy God who died on the cross and was resurrected to save sinners. Hence the covenant creates space for mysteries and marvels unintelligible to human rationality and good sense. So if preaching is an event where *actio divina* and *homo performans* meet,[90] the covenant provides the backdrop for such a preposterous encounter.

The covenant serves as a helpful frame to understand preaching in at least four ways. First, the covenant frames our understanding of the biblical script. The Bible sketches a drama of the Triune God who, from the overflow of love shared in the divine fellowship, initiates an action that "consists of bringing together God and us in beatitude, which is a happiness created by grace in loving communion, or friendship, with God."[91] So, "the *cantus firmus* (melodic theme) of the theodrama is God's single-minded purpose to extend his family: *'covenant establishes kinship.'*"[92] The covenant is a unifying thread that allows us to grasp the continuity and the coherence of the theodramatic story line.

Second, the covenant frames our understanding of God's performance as a meaningful action that has significance *for us* (i.e., it gives us a reason

89. Ivan Patricio Khovacs quotes from Sharon Bailin, "In the Space between the Words: Play Production as an Interpretive Enterprise," *Journal of Aesthetic Education* 35, no. 2 (Summer 2001): 69. See Ivan Patricio Khovacs, "A Cautionary Note on the Use of Theatre for Theology," in *Faithful Performances: Enacting Christian Tradition*, ed. Trevor A. Hart and Steven R. Guthrie (Burlington, VT: Ashgate, 2007), 42.

90. Bartow, *God's Human Speech*, 111.

91. Michael Pasquarello III, *We Speak Because We Have First Been Spoken: A Grammar of the Preaching Life* (Grand Rapids: Eerdmans, 2009), 75.

92. Vanhoozer, *Faith Speaking Understanding*, 102 (emphasis original). Vanhoozer quotes from Scott Hahn, *Kinship through Covenant: A Canonical Approach to the Fulfillment of God's Saving Promises* (New Haven: Yale University Press, 2009), 28.

to perform). The theodrama concerns God's faithfulness and eagerness to grant and guarantee a family relationship with us and to bless us as our eternal God. In other words, the covenant frames the theodrama in a way that we know not only that God has acted in history but also that through his actions we can actually experience and live a different reality. The covenant makes the theodrama pertinent to us.

Third, the covenant frames our understanding of the action we are called to take as we participate in God's drama. Our performance always happens in response to God's speaking and initiating act of love. The story does not begin with or center on us; Scripture reminds us, "You are not your own, for you were bought with a price. So glorify God in your body [i.e., performance]" (1 Cor. 6:19–20).[93] In light of divine love, Christian performance is about the children of God joyfully and faithfully living out the covenantal reality of being invited into his kingdom.

Fourth, the covenant frames how we understand the quality of our relationship with God and with one another. According to Paul, "All this [i.e., the gift of new life] is from God, who through Christ reconciled us to himself and gave us the ministry of reconciliation" (2 Cor. 5:18). The covenant established by Christ's own blood reconciles believers not only to God but also to one another. Hence the relationship between believers should be characterized by a mutual commitment to love, respect, honor, and trust. The covenantal ethic of the church is the display of complete unity. The church's relationship with God should also be characterized by the same kind of commitment to love, respect, honor, and trust. At the same time, God, who is the initiator and establisher of the covenant, is not our equal. God must be revered as the church both dutifully and joyfully submits to God's authority.

The Dress Rehearsal of Corporate Worship

Michael Horton likens worship to a "covenant renewal ceremony" in which people who have been summoned by God gather for a foretaste of

---

93. In this verse, Paul is speaking against sexual immorality, but his charge to "glorify God in your body" applies more broadly to how believers should live (i.e., Christian performance) in light of Christ's sacrifice on their behalf and the presence of the Holy Spirit, who continues to work in them.

the marriage supper of the Lamb.[94] In corporate worship, the covenantal partners (i.e., God and his people) come face to face. Worship is a setting where we remember, reenact, and celebrate the divine-human covenant by praising and glorifying God, who has done great things. Worship is a time of reorientation that allows us to see God, ourselves, one another, and the world in light of the true benevolent and gracious King who has put the burden on himself to bless all creation. Our identity and character are constantly molded in this gathering space, where we are made aware of the story we are a part of and are invited to enact. Although we interpret and perform the drama of salvation in an ongoing cycle of reflection-action in all of life, in worship we remember and rehearse this drama with a heightened awareness of God and others who are called to the same task.

In light of everything we have considered in this chapter, worship may be likened to the church's *dress rehearsal of the theodramatic reality*, where we not only delight in and savor God's glory but also are fashioned for worshipful living both today and in the eschatological future.[95] During the week, the people of God are scattered to diverse settings where each player must improvise the reality of being in Christ at all times. These are the moments of individual rehearsal, where one's faith and personal testimony as a Christian disciple are trained and strengthened through the Spirit's work. Understanding of the biblical script deepens, beliefs and convictions are tested, acting is trained, habits are shaped, and personal faith takes root and grows in the crucible of life, where one daily wrestles with what it means to carry the cross and go after Jesus (Luke 14:27). When Sunday comes, however, all Christian players gather for the dress rehearsal of the theodrama as a team. These moments help God's people remember that we are not alone but are part of a great company—"a cloud of witnesses" (Heb. 12:1)—that subsists on a countercultural imagination of God's kingdom reality.

Our faith is generated through the proclamation of the Word, we are initiated into faith by baptism, and our faith is nourished, preserved,

94. Michael Horton, *A Better Way: Rediscovering the Drama of Christ-Centered Worship* (Grand Rapids: Baker Books, 2002), 24.
95. Debra and Ron Reinstra refer to the fourfold *ordo* of worship (i.e., gathering, proclamation of the Word, the Eucharist, and sending) as "the drama of liturgy" that, "when experienced over and over across many years, it begins to shape a person's soul." See *Worship Words: Disciplining Language for Faithful Ministry* (Grand Rapids: Baker Academic, 2009), 235.

and united through the sacraments. As the church reads and studies the biblical script, assisted by the reflections and insights from the historical church's creeds, confessions, conciliar statements, and lives of saints, we find our place in the larger matrix of the salvific drama and train our imaginations for the role we are to play. In our private and public prayers, praises and confessions, and the fellowship of believers, we not only learn our lines and parts but actually participate and rehearse the theodramatic reality where God is glorified and we are satisfied and united in him. In all this, the Holy Spirit directs and oversees our enactment of the kingdom reality and gets us ready to once again be sent out into the world, where our performance continues. Corporate worship is a dress rehearsal because it bears the closest resemblance to the church's perfected doxological performance in the eternal worship of the Lamb with brothers and sisters from every nation, tribe, people, and language (Rev. 7:9–12). Worship is a proleptic performance of the eschatological glory to come.

In the creative, hospitable space of worship, believers come together and explore questions on life and performance. Questions may range from broad, overarching queries on Christian living to context-specific reflections on what God is putting on the hearts of people. For example: How do we understand and enact this part of the script? How do we express sorrow in the face of tragedy when we know the redemptive ending to the story? How do we rightly convey anger as ones who have been forgiven? How do we rejoice wisely, being aware of others' suffering? In what ways is God challenging our church to better embody Christlike love and sacrifice in this season? What would hope look like in this situation, and how might we personify it?

Considering questions such as these, the church employs the canonical, catholic, and contextual senses to imagine how the theodrama may be fittingly enacted in our families, workplaces, and communities. In the rehearsal space of worship, believers critically reflect on life's questions in light of the gospel and endeavor to respond by living rightly before God and people. Don Saliers describes worship as a school for our imagination of being in the world: "Worship both forms and expresses the faith-experience of the community. Worshipping God involves telling stories, singing praise and trust and hope, sorrow and joy, delight and wonder.

It trains us in lamenting, confessing, adoring, and lifting our cries for the whole world. At its best, Christian worship presents a vision of life created, sustained and redeemed and held in the mystery of grace. *What we do together in acknowledging God 'schools' us in ways of seeing the world and of being in it.*"[96]

Rather than a place where we celebrate perfection and excellence, worship is a liberating space where real people gather before the perfect God to grapple with what it means to live in the world as Christ-followers.[97] In worship "Christians seek in the power of the Spirit to be conformed to the image of Christ—to act like him, think like him, be like him."[98] In worship, the church is drawn into a space of liminality, where the social structure that "holds people apart, defines their differences, and constrains their actions" are suspended and disrupted, so that participants emerge from that experience transformed.[99] Samuel Wells explains that "worship is the time when the conventional rules of the fallen world are suspended," which enables the formation of Christian imagination and character.[100] In these activities, Christ is present in worship through the Spirit, and the church is formed as a doxological community that declares God's praises until the day of Christ's coming.

96. Don E. Saliers, *Worship and Spirituality*, 2nd ed. (Akron, OH: OSL, 1996), 2 (emphasis added).

97. The requirement for excellence and perfection in worship is attributed to God (e.g., the worship is to be excellent *for* God). Worship is the natural duty and privilege of created beings to glorify their Creator and Redeemer, and as such, it is right that the very best of our affections and efforts should be offered to God. Nevertheless, Clayton Schmit asserts, "It is not God who is impressed with human excellence" (*Too Deep for Words: A Theology of Liturgical Expression* [Louisville: Westminster John Knox, 2002], 64). Rather, our pursuit of excellence in worship is not about "God's expectations of us but [about] our expectations of one another and the ways that our modes of expression function" (65). This perception of worship liberates the church to focus on the primary matters of encountering God anew, praising him for who he is, being unified as the body of Christ, and reordering our lives to better embody God's reality in the world.

98. Wells, *Improvisation*, 84.

99. Arnold van Gennep describes three stages to a ritual action: separation, transition, and incorporation. In these "rites of passage," participants detach themselves from past events and identities, and the ritual effects their incorporation into a new life situation. The transitional phase—the space that is "neither here nor there," where the participant is "betwixt and between the positions assigned by law, custom, convention, and ceremonial"—is what Victor Turner refers to as "liminality." Victor Turner, *The Ritual Process: Structure and Anti-Structure* (Chicago: Aldine, 1969), 95; Arnold van Gennep, *The Rites of Passage* (Chicago: University of Chicago Press, 1960).

100. Wells, *Improvisation*, 82.

Conclusion

Scripture is a divinely inspired script that describes a peculiar drama of God's actions in the world. The countercultural drama of God is set in creation, reaches its pinnacle in the cross and resurrection of Jesus Christ, and resolves its denouement in his glorious return. The theodrama—as it moves through time toward the resolution of the fulfillment of God's plan—communicates that there is, indeed, a distinct, unifying meaning to the script as intended by the divine playwright. At the same time, the theodrama has a surplus of meaning, and thus it celebrates diverse renderings of the biblical script by the church. The script of the Bible is intended for enactment.

Preaching is a performance of the theodrama based on the biblical script in interaction with the present context. In engagement with Scripture, the performance tradition of the church, the congregation, and the world, preaching must faithfully and creatively evoke the reality of the theodrama (i.e., the gospel reality). Preaching's purpose is to move people to participate in the theodrama by living out the reality of being in Christ. To this end, preaching reorients people's perspectives and shapes their imaginations so that they see and do reality in light of God's kingdom, which is both here and not yet. In order for the church to embody its role as God's kingdom people in all circumstances, preaching trains believers as skilled improvisers whose rehearsed habits guide their daily performances. Corporate worship is, then, the dress rehearsal in which the entire church participates to practice the theodramatic reality. As the church does so, it always looks forward to the eschatological future, when it will perfectly and eternally dwell in God's kingdom.

6

Four Perspectives at Play within a Theodramatic Homiletic

I n the last several decades, the North American religious scene has been undergoing a theological paradigm shift because of displacement of the philosophical tectonic plates on which we Americans have built our religious lives. Moving away from the epistemic foundationalism of modernity, which upholds the notion of indisputable and independently existing truth, many people are turning to the holism of postmodernity, insisting that knowledge functions as a system created by interconnection with others. In this book, I have sought to examine the ways this philosophical shift is manifested in the contrasting approaches of the traditional homiletic and the conversational homiletic and to propose theodramatic homiletic as a third, centric approach that addresses their pitfalls and draws on their strengths. This study has investigated the assumptions and approaches of the two prevalent preaching models in our day and presented dramatic theology to bridge the two preaching extremes. The traditional and conversational models not only are two distinct approaches to sermons but also represent the two ends of a spectrum on which preaching styles can be located and reflected on in light of the corrections offered by the dramatic model.

Four Distinctives of a Theodramatic Homiletic

Four lines of thought contribute to the distinctiveness of a theodramatic homiletic. *First, a theodramatic homiletic invites the church to confidently cling to the uniqueness of the gospel while not losing our humility as situated knowers.* Theodramatic preaching does not subscribe to the postmodern despair and disillusionment, embodied in the conversational model, about language, authority, and, more broadly, a singular reality. Instead, it operates from assurance in the revelation of Scripture, which conveys to us a grand unifying drama of God pregnant with meaning and significance that can be identified and understood—and that we can respond to. Unlike the conversational homiletic, which denies a discernible meaning of Scripture, the theodramatic model maintains that the biblical discourse makes God known to us through his names, attributes, and actions. God makes himself known in creation, Israel's history, and the story of the early church but most clearly and definitively in the person and work of Jesus Christ. Yet we must couple this hermeneutical confidence with the acknowledgment of divine incomprehensibility—that God can never be exhaustively known—and that in our human limitations we cannot arrive at the final meaning of Scripture. Scripture is not a fixed text in which one static meaning is embedded; it has a surplus of meaning that is far "richer than any literal paraphrase."[1] Both at the level of sentences and in the canon as a whole, the Bible has a "polyphonic circulation of meaning, exceeding the capacity of any one of the individual discourses."[2] So a theodramatic homiletic encourages preachers to diligently make sense of what God is saying and doing through the Scriptures in our world, even as we withhold past assumptions, remain open to pushback and revisions, and welcome diverse and fresh understandings of the biblical script that emerge with each performance. The theodramatic model strives to deftly uphold both constancy and provisionality in interpretations that preserve both the integrity of Scripture and the integrity of readers.

1. Kevin J. Vanhoozer, "God's Mighty Speech-Acts: The Doctrine of Scripture Today," in *Pathway into the Holy Scripture*, ed. P. E. Satterthwaite and D. F. Wright (Grand Rapids: Eerdmans, 1994), 172.
2. Timothy Ward, "The Diversity and Sufficiency of Scripture," in *The Trustworthiness of God: Perspectives on the Nature of Scripture*, ed. Paul Helm and Carl R. Trueman (Grand Rapids: Eerdmans, 2002), 211.

Second, a theodramatic homiletic invites the preacher and the congregation to the theodrama as equal participants because the church as a whole is a theater of the gospel. The work of discerning God's Word in the present context and performing that Word on the stage of the world is a shared responsibility of the preacher and the congregation. The faith community must work as a theater company that critically reflects on a fitting enactment of the biblical script by employing the canonical, catholic, and contextual senses.[3] Being attentive to the biblical canon, Christian tradition, and the present context, the preacher and the congregation collectively engage various "texts" available to them in order to make sense of God's uninterrupted action in the world.

What is the role of preaching in the relationship between the preacher and the congregation? Preaching constitutes a primary way in which believers engage one another and nurture faithful imagination for Christian performance. Preaching is the performance of the theodrama that inspires other performances that submit to God's Word. The sermon is the preacher's performance of the theodrama inasmuch as it is the preacher who, as the appointed voice of the community, models faith that sees reality in relation to the gospel. Nonetheless, the sermon is not just the preacher's but also a corporate expression of faith of the entire church. Since interpretive performance is the work of all people of God, the sermon rises from and in the midst of the common life of the church, even as it is a word that we receive from God, mediated by Scripture. Believers also commit to living as agents of transformation in the world. The preacher acts as an interpretive leader who demonstrates for the congregation how to process different texts available to the church (e.g., the Bible, church tradition, stories/testimonies of believers, world events) and, through that, discerns with the church God's action in the present moment in order for the church to join in. By emphasizing "the playerhood of all believers,"[4] a theodramatic homiletic identifies neither with the traditional model (which elevates the preacher over the congregation) nor with the conversational model (which risks obscuring distinct roles and gifts within the body of Christ). In the theodramatic model, the preacher functions as a director

3. Kevin J. Vanhoozer, *The Drama of Doctrine: A Canonical-Linguistic Approach to Christian Theology* (Louisville: Westminster John Knox, 2005), 205.
4. Vanhoozer, *Drama of Doctrine*, 414.

who supervises the local church's performance by making the script more accessible to the actors through interpretive leadership that engages them as agent-subjects.

Third, a theodramatic homiletic invites the church to actively partici-pate in God's mission in the world. The purpose of theodramatic preaching is to help the church hear and respond to God by bearing witness to his re-creating ministry that is unfolding in and all around us, in Christ through the Spirit. Preaching inspires and prompts the church to enact this reality of the gospel in joyful obedience by understanding and living out our identity of being "in Christ" until the day of his return. The church is a peculiar people whose identity and worldview are shaped by the countercultural gospel. As such, the church sees things not simply as they appear but as they really are before God—the reality of the Triune God's outworking of salvation in the past, present, and future—for the sake of his glory, which is acclaimed by our adoration. Preaching as a Christian performance enacts this reality and models speech and action shaped by the divine drama. In doing so, it forms Christian improvisers who know the biblical script by heart, are rooted in tradition, and can adapt to the changing contexts with agility so that they can, in all times and places, embody their roles as ones united to Christ.

By envisioning preaching as a ministry that incites the church to act, the theodramatic model hopes to restore what Augustine designated as the third and overarching aspect of preaching's purpose—to *move* the listeners to action. As Thomas Long observes, the Western pulpit has concentrated its effort on the task of *teaching* for many centuries.[5] Sermons have been perceived primarily as a pedagogical activity with the objective of inculcating knowledge in listeners. With the rise of the New Homiletic, the pulpit's interest has, by and large, shifted to *delighting*, as ministers have sought to evoke a deeply personal and inspirational experience for the listeners. This change can be seen in the conversational model's emphasis on creating a communal space through a sermon where the members can savor and share their experience of the text. A theodramatic homiletic revives and recommits to preaching's task of *moving*

---

5. Thomas Long, *Preaching from Memory to Hope* (Louisville: Westminster John Knox, 2009), 17–18.

the church to live in the fullness of the gospel by loving God and loving our neighbors.

Fourth, a theodramatic homiletic invites the church to grasp the broad scope of God's dramatic action. Alasdair MacIntyre once said, "I can only answer the question, 'What am I to do?' if I can answer the prior question, 'Of what story do I find myself a part?'"[6] Our individual and collective stories are subsumed and find meaning in the biblical drama about creation; Israel; the life, death, resurrection, and ascension of Jesus Christ; the community of his disciples; and the complete transformation of the whole creation. The Scriptures portray an uninterrupted outworking of God's salvation in history, and this is the lens from which we must understand God, who continues to be faithfully present in and through the church, moving toward a dramatic resolution to his story with Christ's triumphal second coming.

Knowing our parts to enact in this drama requires understanding the full range of the Triune God's actions in his whole story, rather than reading the Bible as sundry fragmented texts. In light of the biblical drama, hermeneutics and preaching according to a theodramatic homiletic will convey the continuity of divine speech and action in the past and the present so that the whole church can act in congruence with God's ordained goal, plan, and mission for cosmic renewal. Preaching helps believers find themselves within the theodrama and see their lives as the epicenter of divine activity: God is doing something in and around us; God works freely and independently of us but delights to involve us in his story.

Maintaining a full-range perspective of God's dramatic action is an essential characteristic of the theodramatic model. A danger of the traditional homiletic is an emphasis on the significance of God's past actions in the static meaning of a historical composition of the text. The pitfall of the conversational homiletic is a narrow focus on the church's present experience. Theodramatic preaching, however, emphasizes the remembrance of God's historic and future actions told by Scripture and allows that future-oriented memory to guide our reflection and enactment of God's at-this-moment work.

---

6. Alasdair MacIntyre, *After Virtue* (Notre Dame, IN: University of Notre Dame Press, 1981), 216.

Four Perspectives in a Theodramatic Homiletic

The remainder of this chapter explores four practice-shaping perspectives that help us be mindful of the whole divine drama and our contexts in preaching. These perspectives are retrospection, introspection, extrospection, and prospection. Wesley Vander Lugt notes that to perform the biblical drama, we need "theodramatic disponibility," which is "the comprehensive availability of an actor in the theodrama whose character is formed by . . . various dispositions [e.g., trinitarian, biblical, ecclesial, traditional, missional, and contextual] and consequently is ready to participate faithfully in the theodrama."[7] Such disponibility is cultivated by "attentiveness to and awareness of the triune God, Scripture, the church, tradition, unbelievers, and local contexts."[8] The four perspectives may be thought of as practices that train us to be attentive to the full account of God's story and aware of the contexts where we must perform the reality of being in Christ. It has been stated a number of times already that theodramatic preaching comes to form in a lively interaction with a variety of "texts," including Scripture, theology, church tradition, the stories and lives of present believers, and current events around the world. On this point, we may also think of the four perspectives as ways to develop the canonical, catholic, and contextual senses that help us discern and make sense of God's activities in the world so we can play a role in his mission. This is an interdisciplinary approach to preaching that relies on a wide range of "academic" and "experiential" theological courses, as well as nonclassical seminary courses that today are part of many curricula that train ministers (e.g., counseling, psychology, intercultural studies). Our main interest in this discussion is not the need for better integration in theological education or better demonstration of how it can be done, though both are important. The four perspectives show both that various disciplines can come together in preaching and that, together, they provide rich resources that strengthen our theological reflection and performance. As Barth says, "Theology as a church discipline

---

7. Wesley Vander Lugt, *Living Theodrama: Reimagining Theological Ethics* (Burlington, VT: Ashgate, 2014), 40.

8. Vander Lugt, *Living Theodrama*, 47. See Vander Lugt's work for a rich discussion on how theodramatic disponibility may be developed.

ought in all its branches to be nothing other than sermon preparation in the broadest sense."[9]

Two points of clarification may be helpful. First, the four perspectives are not a step-by-step methodology for sermon development or a pragmatic preaching strategy to effect a desired change. They are, rather, practices of attentiveness and awareness of the full scope of divine actions in the past, present, and future, underwritten by dramatic theology of Scripture, which can be complemented by other exegetical-homiletical approaches. As such, the aim of the four perspectives is to remember divine initiative, agency, and action so we can posture ourselves as servants addressed by the authoritative divine Word instead of using Scripture in preaching to fulfill our needs and agendas. These practices cultivate a life of prayerful response to God who graciously enacts renewal in creation through the sacrifice of his Son by the means of the Spirit.

Second, these four perspectives do not compose a new homiletic model; rather, they represent the theological practices of past and present-day preachers who are committed to making known the fullness of the gospel in the trinitarian theology of the biblical narrative. A danger of the critique of "traditional preaching" by some New Homiletic advocates is a skewed generalization of the pulpit's legacy that results in a problematic logic that today we need new innovative preaching models. The implication is that our predecessors of faith have largely missed the mark, so to speak, for nearly two thousand years, and preaching needs to be "fixed."[10] However, a theodramatic homiletic is not an inventive, original approach to sermons but simply preaching that calls for attentiveness to the internal logic, consistency, and shape of the Scriptures that witness to God revealed in Jesus Christ. Many exemplars have preached this way in the past, and many still do so today.[11] The four perspectives are practices for a life shaped

---

9. Karl Barth, *Homiletics*, trans. Geoffrey W. Bromiley and Donald E. Daniels (Louisville: Westminster John Knox, 1991), 17.

10. See David J. Lose, *Preaching at the Crossroads: How the World—and Our Preaching—Is Changing* (Minneapolis: Fortress, 2013), 1–9.

11. Jesus is the master teacher who spoke in this way and connected God's will and plan communicated in the Torah and the Old Testament prophesies to himself, who realizes and fulfills them. We have a memorable example in Luke 24:13–35, where Jesus travels with two downcast disciples on the road to Emmaus and, "beginning with Moses and all the Prophets, he interpreted to them in all the Scriptures the things concerning himself" (v. 27). The narrative ends with the disciples' despair transformed into joy and a renewed sense of mission, as they are reoriented

by Scripture, prayer, praise, and the communion of saints that train us to drink continuously from God's new mercies and graces to be formed and reformed into a holy community that declares God's glory in our speech and action. They are helpful guides in the preacher's study, meditation, and performance of Scripture and in the church's shared task as a theater of the gospel, which spurs one another on toward maturity in Christ.

Retrospection: Attentiveness to God's Historical Actions

Retrospection is attentiveness to God's past actions in the theodrama. Retrospective work most significantly involves reading and studying Scripture to learn about the Triune God, who reveals himself to us in it and in the economy of salvation, but it includes more. Broadly speaking, retrospection considers what God has done so far in history, and thus it reflects on the salvation history depicted in Scripture and continued in

---

to Jerusalem as witnesses of the resurrected Christ, who made their hearts burn as he opened the Scriptures to them. The Old Testament prophets preached the covenantal story of "the God of Abraham, Isaac, and Jacob" that creates and sustains the identity, lifeway, and purpose of the people of Israel. This grand narrative of divine grace, which was not only for them but includes all nations, reminds them where they come from and who they are called to be among the nations in light of the coming Messiah, and that was the lens used by the prophets to make sense of Israel's and Judah's circumstances and to deliver oracles of judgment and hope. Peter's sermon at Solomon's Portico after healing a lame man in Acts 3:11–26 also sketches the drama of redemption of "the God of Abraham, the God of Isaac, and the God of Jacob, and the God of our fathers, glorified in his servant Jesus," whom—though they denied him and delivered him to die—God raised from the dead. Peter proclaimed that it is this Jesus, the "Holy and Righteous One," "the Author of Life," who healed the lame man. Although Stephen's sermon, found in Acts 7:1–53, was perhaps cut short by his death, it is clear that his preaching was supported by a dramatic understanding of God's unifying story and his desire to bless the world through the "coming of the Righteous One," before whom the world stands accountable and shall be judged for rejecting (Acts 7:1–53). Paul, too, "preaches" in his letter to the Ephesians by sketching a cosmic picture of God's reconciling work in Christ that unites us to God and to one another by the gift of faith through divine grace. See Timothy G. Gombis, *The Drama of Ephesians: Participating in the Triumph of God* (Downers Grove, IL: InterVarsity Press, 2010). Another example worth mentioning here is Augustine, since his theology and practice of preaching have commonly been misportrayed to fit the traditional homiletic. Augustine's *City of God* is not a sermon in a strict sense, but his philosophical treatise exhibits a similar quality as the sermons described above; he gives a breathtaking interpretation of human history and the state of the world in relation to the universal tale of two opposing cities—the city of God formed by love of God, even to the disregard of self, and the city of Earth formed by self-love, even to the disregard of God—and the church that lives as a community of faithful pilgrims on the way to their heavenly home. Augustine, *City of God*, ed. David Knowles, trans. Henry Bettenson (New York: Pelican Books, 1972). See also Michael Pasquarello III, "Augustine of Hippo," in *Sacred Rhetoric: Preaching as a Theological and Pastoral Practice of the Church* (Grand Rapids: Eerdmans, 2005).

the church's past story of faith. For this reason, retrospection is aided by disciplines like biblical theology, systematic theology,[12] creedal theology, and historical theology. Simply put, this is the kind of work commonly associated with seminary education and the strength of the traditional homiletic: acquiring Hebrew and Greek language skills to exegete passages; studying the biblical background, history, literary styles, and theological themes of each book; learning about the church's past and the development of historical creeds, conciliar statements, and confessions; and reflecting on the biblical canon as one coherent unit that is responsible for ongoing theological construction. Retrospection is foundational and vital in sermon preparation.

Retrospective work relies on those skills and knowledge and includes examining various aspects of a text so that we can humbly enter God's story and tune our ears to what God once said to his people. For example, a pastor preparing a sermon should investigate the historical context by reflecting on the biblical passage in its historical setting, as it was meant for its original audience. You may consider questions such as, Who is the author of this text? Who is it written for? What are the nature, occasion, and purpose of the writing? What do we know about the text's geographic, topographical, and sociocultural background, and how are they significant to this text? What ancient customs and practices or literary expressions are referred to in the passage, and what are their meaning and significance? Again, our aim in asking these questions is to get a sense of the situation to which God through the human author was speaking.

The pastor should also probe the literary context by observing textual-linguistic features that shed light on what the biblical author is saying and doing through the text. What is the text's genre? What are the indications that the boundaries set for the text mark one coherent unit of thought? What are notable textual and/or translation issues? How are

---

12. Strictly speaking, systematic theology, which is concerned with the significance of the biblical canon as it applies to doctrines that guide our faithful performance today, does not belong to the retrospective category alone but rather undergirds all four perspectives. In other words, doctrinal theology guides how we ought to live today in light of God's deeds and promises in the past and future. The statement above therefore points to a common misunderstanding of theology's task and the misbalance in seminary education and preaching courses if only these theological disciplines are emphasized, precluding practical theological disciplines and resources in the other three perspectives to follow.

English translations (or translations in the preacher's preferred language) similar and different on this text? What is the text's structure and movement? How does the passage fit into the larger organization of the book? Who are the characters in the passage? What is the tension or conflict, and how is it depicted? Is resolution offered? (If not, why might this be, and how does the text end instead?) What kinds of literary tools does the author use in this text (e.g., symbolism, alliteration, hyperbole, metaphor, simile, synecdoche, repetition)? What role do the literary features play in the text? What key words stand out (i.e., note their range of meaning, occurrences in other texts, historical and theological significance, and how they enhance this text)? What is the theme of the text? These questions help us grasp what a passage is saying (and not saying!). This important work enables us to read individual pericopes in the proper context of whole books, letters, or sets of writing (e.g., the Gospels) and tune our ears to not only *what* the original author intended but also *how* the author communicated it.

The pastor is also encouraged to think about the theological significance of the text, reflecting on the overarching biblical and doctrinal themes present in the passage. Questions here may include, What does the text say about God (or humanity, creation, sin, salvation, church, judgment)? How does this text relate to the biblical canon? What themes in this text are developed and woven throughout the Bible? How does this passage advance God's story, which comes to a climax in the life and ministry of Jesus Christ? What claim does the text make on us today so we can partake in the future made possible through Christ? What teaching of the church is represented in the text? How has this text been interpreted by early church fathers and mothers and other believers through history? What confessions, creeds, or catechisms of the church resonate with the text? The aim here is to situate the passage and our study and interpretation of it in the larger context of the biblical drama and to converse about them with diverse thinkers throughout the church's past.

We engage in retrospection by carefully considering God's historical acts testified to by Scripture, aided by the church's theological heritage and wisdom that function as signposts to guide our contemplation. In order to understand our place and role in God's drama, we begin by getting a sense of the story we must enact, such as what it is about, what it is *not*, the story line and significant developments, other characters, key themes, and literary techniques that are used to communicate the story in all its richness. Through these, the preacher first aims to see that "the God who acts in the Old Testament is the God who becomes flesh in the New Testament in order to achieve the definitive saving work in the world"[13] and, second, to understand the divine playwright's overarching intention in the theodrama to unite all things to Christ so that we can align our performances with his creative vision. The goal of retrospection is to deeply understand not only a select sermon text and its historical particularity but also how that text stands in relation to the whole biblical drama. Retrospective work also considers how other believers have understood the biblical script and how they enacted their parts. Along with the Holy Spirit who guides us, we are "surrounded by so great a cloud of witnesses" (Heb. 12:1) who have gone before us. The ways they understood and inhabited the same story serve as our living examples, conversational partners, and "rule of faith" that inform our performance. At the same time, retrospection should also be done with present believers, who constitute the local church. In this partnership, pastors should draw on their gifts, training, and knowledge from their personal study to lead these conversations, while inviting the church as a company of actors to join in and share insights and reflections that deepen and refresh the understanding of the biblical script. These discussions may take place in various forms and places, such as Sunday schools, Bible study gatherings, small groups, pre-sermon meetings, and casual meetings with members. What matters is that as the preacher and the congregation alike enact the theodrama in their daily lives, the performance understandings that they bring to bear on a given passage should be shared to enrich their conversations.

Retrospection is integral to the preservation of the Christian memory. The acts of recalling and retrieving are crucial to not lose, forget, or allow what is central to Christian theology to get distorted with time and distance. The epic in the theodrama grounds our performance in the biblical canon and allows us to be consistent with it. Knowledge of what has happened so far in the story also helps us know our parts and fully commit

13. Graeme Goldsworthy, *Preaching the Whole Bible as Christian Scripture: The Application of Biblical Theology to Expository Preaching* (Grand Rapids: Eerdmans, 2000), 6.

to acting them today with flexibility and adaptability. Retrospection keeps our performance of the theodrama not only accountable and conforming to Scripture but also congruent with the past ecclesial performance, which may be resourced and refocused in our time.

Retrospection is unproductive and futile without the other three perspectives, however. Retrospection runs the danger of a narrow focus on a single text that makes it difficult for listeners to grasp how it fits into the larger biblical narrative. This limitation can result in sermons that—while informative and interesting, with impressive exegetical-hermeneutical content—do not effectively move people to action because the significance of the information is unclear in relation to them, and it does not speak to their present experience of being in the world.

Introspection: Attentiveness to God's Present Action in Us

Introspection considers what God is doing today through the ministry of the Holy Spirit *in us*. As pastors read and meditate on Scripture in sermon preparation, they should engage with the text in a way that leads them to honestly examine their spiritual, mental, emotional, physical, and social state of being in the world. If the driving interest of retrospection is discovering the historical meaning of the text, introspection and extrospection are concerned with the "present meaning" of the text that is being progressively fulfilled today through God's ongoing work in us and in the world, respectively.

We depend on the Holy Spirit to see ourselves truthfully in relation to Scripture, and we reference our received tradition and the living examples of saints in the process. But in addition we may use resources from counseling, psychology, sociology, and other social sciences to name and clarify our understanding of the inner workings, stories, behavioral patterns, and systems that make up who we are. Scripture alone is the authoritative Word that can pronounce the verdict of our state, assess our condition as creatures, and make a determinant claim about our lives, so our engagement with the Bible does not end with retrospection, even though we do not rule out other tools here. Introspection is a way of prayerfully attuning ourselves to the Spirit, who applies Christ's redemptive work on the cross in our lives, so we ask that he would "search [us] . . . know [our] heart[s]" so that our inner life turns from "any grievous way" and follows "the way everlasting" (Ps. 139:23–24).

As conversational preachers have asserted, human beings are not neutral interpreters who approach the Bible as blank slates. We bring to the reading of Scripture and to preaching our presuppositions, beliefs, and expectations, which are fashioned by our experiences as beings in time and space who are connected to others. Introspection forces us to honestly face our own biases, failures, prejudices, sins, addictions, injustices, fears, and limitations. At the same time, through such self-examination we become aware of our strengths, gifts and abilities, turning points, potential, and changes in our habits and character that point to God's persistent transforming work in us. In short, the process of introspection allows us to see ourselves in light of the theodrama and become caught up in it so that our faith performance wells up as a response of gratitude and worship to God. As ones saved by grace and now in Christ Jesus, we constantly strive to "live according to the Spirit" and "set [our] minds on the things of the Spirit" (Rom. 8:5).

Because introspection involves who we are as complex spiritual, emotional, physical, and social beings before God, we can consider many types of questions in order to personally appropriate the text: In what ways do I identify with the text? What parts do I find difficult to connect with? How does the passage speak to my fears, anger, hurts, and despair? How does it speak to my ideals, hopes, and dreams? How does this text affirm, challenge, and/or reorient my view of God, others, and myself? What personal response or commitment does this text demand from me? How does this text reorder my view of body, health, and physical comfort? What does this passage say about human suffering? How does this text help me understand my race, ethnicity, and gender? How does this text challenge the role my finances and possessions play in Christian discipleship? How does the world behind the text parallel the systems and cultures that I am part of today? How does my life reflect God's character of justice, love, forgiveness, peacemaking, and hospitality to those near and far? How do I show discrimination, injustice, and intolerance? How do I help those around me know God revealed in Jesus Christ? How might God be working in my life at this time to make me more like Christ? Is my life bearing the fruit of the Spirit?

All these examples show that personal and lyrical participation in the theodrama is indispensable to the hermeneutical and homiletical task because we are active participants of its reality. Even though the task in this stage is self-examination, the basis for inward reflection, change, and action is not us but God's holiness, which judges and builds us up as his holy people through the unification and regeneration of the Spirit.

The homiletical literature of our time shows a diminished interest in introspection as an integral task in preaching. Pastors' holiness, virtue, and matters of their hearts and personal lives were common topics in sermon manuals of old—explored extensively with a sense of urgency and vigor as though our integrity as Christ's disciples and fruitfulness of long-term ministry depended on them—but they occupy little space and weight in modern preaching literature. This may be because these topics seem self-evident and trite, and preachers presumably already know what they should be doing. Yet with the Spirit's guidance and our genuine effort, an honest assessment and awareness of our inner world is paramount for our relationship with God and our vitality in life and ministry. This should not be seen as an individual's task; the minister should solicit help from trusted family members, friends, colleagues, and congregation members who can speak truth in love. This should also be a shared task of the body of Christ.

Introspection is important for at least three reasons. First, it allows preachers to view themselves and their lives as belonging to the theodrama and as part of God's renewing ministry that is also extended to them. God's kingdom drama is unfolding not only "out there" in the world but also within each of us, inviting us to more deeply and fully participate in the divine life. As ministers of the gospel, we preach Christ to all who need to be forgiven and saved to enjoy the Creator's gift of abundant life—including to ourselves. Introspection is vital to preaching because through this process Scripture becomes personal to us.

Second, introspection allows preachers to get in touch with their humanity and speak authentically to connect with the congregation as fellow human beings. If Charles Bartow is right that the task of preaching is turning ink into blood,[14] the process of introspection takes a step closer

---

14. Bartow is playing off T. S. Eliot's famous saying that literature's purpose is to "turn blood into ink." Charles Bartow, *God's Human Speech: A Practical Theology of Proclamation* (Grand Rapids: Eerdmans, 1997), 63.

toward that goal of relaying the incarnational Word to the church. Along with extrospection, which we will discuss next, introspection develops our contextual sensitivity.

Third, through introspection, preachers can discover their "preaching voice," which is not just a matter of vocal sound but also a deep expression of Christian integrity, delight, freedom, and self-discovery in the Spirit. Breaking away from a compulsive need to mimic the preaching styles of others (vs. healthy aspiration to learn from others), introspection trains preachers to be fully in their own skin, sit in the tensions of their own lives, own every part of their story, and, in the midst of it all, find that God is present right where they are and is doing a new thing.

The danger of introspection, if it is not combined with the other three perspectives, is that one can easily get absorbed in a "me and Jesus" kind of spirituality that diminishes God's drama of cosmic redemption into a private story of individual salvation and sanctification. Also, sermons produced purely by introspection may emotionally connect with listeners, but in the end, people have little to go on without a clear "word from God" from Scripture that forms and nourishes them. Or they are driven to try harder to become better on their own without the gospel that exposes the lies of the enemy and gives them genuine hope. Yet when introspection is done carefully in prayer with Scripture in the fellowship of believers, it helps us internalize the theodrama through instruction of our minds and connection to our hearts, propelling us to go out to the world.

Extrospection: Attentiveness to God's Present Action around Us

Extrospection is attentiveness to God's present work *in the world*. Specifically, two contexts should be considered: local and global. In order to understand these contexts, we may find that the tools of sociology, anthropology, intercultural studies, evangelism, missiology, and leadership studies particularly benefit our engagement with Scripture. Through Christ's reconciling work on the cross, God's kingdom is here, impinging on our world and ordinary lives. Even though death, brokenness, and evil seem rampant, God's kingdom is visible if we look carefully: lives are being converted; hearts once filled with vitriol are learning to embrace mercy, forgiveness, and love; selfless acts of kindness and compassion are being carried out in Jesus's name; joy and peace are being experienced in unimaginable circumstances; people are courageously confronting evil and injustice for Christ's sake; and fundamental reorderings of life's ideals, goals, and purpose are taking place all over the world. God continues to redeem and conserve the world for the consummation of his plan. Engaging Scripture and the grammar of Christian doctrines, extrospection contemplates God's ongoing story—how "the word of the truth, the gospel, which has come to [us]" is "indeed in the whole world . . . bearing fruit and increasing" (Col. 1:5–6). Pondering the wonders of God's saving and sanctifying work today and witnessing to his faithful and loving presence in redeeming and conserving the world is an important practice that allows us to conform not only to *what* God is doing but also with *how* God is at work. A critical reflection on God's performance in the world and the global church's participation in God's ongoing story allow us to evaluate, expand, and, as needed, even adjust our understanding of Scripture and our performances.

Being mindful of God's presence in the local context of preaching begins by paying attention to the congregational culture. This includes paying attention to our members and their stories, beliefs, values, and practices; the history and tradition of the faith community; and local and national forces that exert influence on this group. Helpful in this regard is Leonora Tubbs Tisdale's suggestion that preachers act as amateur cultural anthropologists who observe and process "thick" descriptions about various symbols in the congregational culture.[15] Whereas "thin" descriptions provide only a basic account about the observable symbols in a congregational culture (e.g., "There is little female presence on the stage in Sunday worship"), "thick" description involves the interpretations of symbols and their meanings as perceived and used by the participants in the culture (e.g., "The church's complementarian stance on the issue of women and ministry translates into preferring male leadership in worship").[16] The preacher as an amateur ethnographer should be a participant-observer who understands the church's culture with all of its layers of complexity.[17]

15. Leonora Tubbs Tisdale, *Preaching as Local Theology and Folk Art* (Minneapolis: Fortress, 1997), 56.

16. Tisdale, *Preaching as Local Theology*, 58.

17. This is similar to what leadership experts Ronald A. Heifetz and Marty Linsky suggest as maintaining a "balcony perspective" that requires proximity and distance from the group.

The preacher needs to study various "symbols," but Tisdale names seven that are essential: stories and interviews of people; archival materials (e.g., minutes of meetings, financial records, pictures, worship bulletins); demographics (e.g., actual and targeted demographics); architecture and visual arts (e.g., use of space, decorations, designs of posters); rituals (e.g., baptisms, communion, weddings, funerals); events and activities (e.g., annual youth missions, community services, Sunday school classes); and people (e.g., Who is at the center/margin?).[18] These symbols provide a window into the congregation's history, cherished beliefs, assumptions, spoken and unspoken rules of conduct, ideals, relational dynamics, loyalties, and views of God and one another. In addition to these symbols, preachers should also consider what is happening in their neighborhood, community, and even the nation at large. This means taking note of demographic statistics, racial/ethnic relations, cultural character and the "feel" of the community, social problems (e.g., regarding race, drugs, crime), and economic or political realities.[19]

By examining such things, the preacher engages in extrospection. The preacher can then partner with the members of the congregation to reflect on the sermon text in light of how God might be moving among them. Together, preacher and congregation can assess whether their present faith performance (individual and collective) appropriately represents the reality of God's in-breaking presence in the world: How does the text before us shed new light on our context? How is our world similar to and unlike the world behind the text? What human needs, desires, fears, and hopes are captured in this text, and how do we see that played out in our world? What do we know about God from this text? How is God continuing his work in our day? Where is our congregation currently failing to live by the script? Where are we succeeding? What hope and promise does this text convey that give us the strength to take a step toward change? How does Christ's redemptive work shape the way we see our congregation, neighborhoods, and communities?

See Ronald A. Heifetz and Marty Linsky, *Leadership on the Line: Staying Alive through the Dangers of Leading* (Boston: Harvard Business School, 2000), 53.

18. Tisdale, *Preaching as Local Theology*, 64–77.

19. See James Henry Harris, "Interpreting the Larger Social Context," in *Teaching Preaching as a Christian Practice: A New Approach to Homiletical Pedagogy*, ed. Thomas G. Long and Leonora Tubbs Tisdale (Louisville: Westminster John Knox, 2008), 90–99.

Extrospection opens up space for preacher and congregation to faithfully imagine how they might participate fully in what God is doing ahead of them in the world. How can they contribute to the central conversations in their local community and nation? The goal here is to make sense of our place in God's world and recalibrate our words and actions in light of our reflection. Deliberation of this kind matters for two reasons. First, preaching is, and should always be, thoroughly practical, stemming from and fostering a dialectical unity between knowing and being. Second, preaching not only proclaims to the congregation but also rises out of the congregational culture and should speak on their behalf. If preacher and congregation investigate how their attitudes and actions represent Jesus, then sermons can be a contextual performance that will stimulate people's longing for and thinking toward a mission-shaped life.

Extrospection, however, does not stop with the church's locality; it ponders the *global* work of God. This is the second aspect of extrospection: grasping a worldwide vision of the kingdom of God by turning to the experiences of Christian brothers and sisters scattered around the globe. In heeding their voices, we do not simply hope to see the world through their eyes so that our understanding of God and the gospel are enhanced. This is true and important, but the reason is much more fundamental: we are one redeemed people, one body of Christ that is being formed together to showcase God's glory. Our faith performance is not complete without one another. The global church participates in the same story, and we must act as one united company of faithful improvisers in the world. God's grand redemptive plan is being fulfilled on the world's stage, and our participation in God's advancing mission must remember and accord with our interdependence.

Considering the global state of the church is not easy and requires wisdom and sensitivity. The "world church" is complex—it captures multiracial, multiethnic, multinational, multilingual, and multicontextual multitudes. In light of this complexity, the experience of the global church resists simplification. Moreover, many of the stories from the majority-world church require sensitivity and sympathy to issues of human rights, freedom, safety, justice, race, and gender. So turning to the experience of the global church requires our willingness to listen to and learn from others' experiences without usurping their stories or projecting our worldview onto them. In Christian humility, solidarity, and love, we tune our ears to their voices, lament with them, celebrate with them, and, most of all, learn from them.

With the Bible as our script, the Spirit as our director, and fellow Christians as our teachers, our churches should consider how believers from other parts of the world understand a certain text. We can ask, What does it mean to be Christians in their contexts? How do they understand the gospel and see it being realized in and around them? What are their greatest stories of delight? What motivates and moves them? How are we adding to their joy? What obstacles and challenges to faith have they faced? What patterns of their society and culture do they find antithetical and antagonistic to the gospel? How are we contributing to those issues (e.g., systemic injustice, segregation, violence, apathy, and indifference)? How do they understand the Holy Spirit's activities in their culture and society? What glimpses of divine goodness and hope do they see in their parts of the world? How can we partner with what God is doing in their region of the world? What would they like for us to learn from their modeling of faith? Specific questions will vary, but the underlying aim is to stand united with the worldwide church and allow our understanding of God and Scripture to be stretched, challenged, and corrected so our performance corresponds with and points to God's performance on the world's stage.

Attentiveness to God's present action in us (introspection) and around us (extrospection) is insufficient without Scripture's witness of Christ, but joined with retrospection, these two perspectives help us understand our stories along the continuum of the theodrama. Also, although all four perspectives at play in a theodramatic homiletic emphasize reading Scripture "with the whole church" (i.e., the living tradition of past and present believers) and thus requires the development of catholic sensitivity, extrospection highlights this importance further. The danger of extrospection if it is not done with the other three perspectives is that we can focus on doing good works without being rooted in divine grace that is the basis for right deeds. Heavily extrospective sermons tend to be moralistic, change driven, and program oriented, with slim theology that does not sufficiently engage the meaning and purpose behind our actions or expose and renew our motives. Sermons of this kind can rally the congregation around a vision or a cause and animate them to act initially, but they do not effectively impel people to keep fighting the good fight (1 Tim. 6:12) or remind them from where they have fallen so they can do the works they did at first (Rev. 2:5). Therefore, the themes that emerge from introspection and extrospection about our inner world and the external world should not dictate the sermon's direction or compose the sermon's central content; preaching is not self-help talk, therapeutic motivational speech, or social advocacy for change. The church gathers around Scripture to hear from the holy God. The principal role of introspection and extrospection is to make us behold God, who is at work in us, among us, and around us, enacting his story of salvation and sanctification for all creation, so we may align ourselves with his ways and go out to the world in Christ's name.

Prospection: Attentiveness to God's Future Action

Prospection is the act of "remembering the future,"[20] in which we reflect on the unfinished story of God and Scripture's promises about God's kingdom that is "not yet" here. With such reflection, this knowledge allows us to live as mature children of God in wisdom—preparing, proclaiming, and participating in what God is bringing to consummation with Christ's return. Coupled with retrospection, the practice of prospection cultivates our canonical sense for Christian performance. In this work, biblical studies, doctrinal theology, systematic theology, and missiology primarily guide our thinking.

Our general reticence to talk about eschatology makes it one of the most overlooked topics in preaching today. "The language of an eschatological future, now turned to vapor, [is] sucked up into the engine of the optimistic present tense, and mainstream American preachers, deprived of eschatological language, devoid of future hope, became instead apostles of progress in many forms—moral progress, social improvement, the 'power of positive thinking,' church growth, and the psychotherapeutic gospel."[21]

Without eschatology, however, our faith and preaching are incomplete. Despite differences in our interpretations about the details surrounding the last things, our shared hope in Christ unifies and compels us. Moreover,

---

20. Don E. Saliers, *Worship as Theology: A Foretaste of Glory Divine* (Nashville: Abingdon, 1994), 217.

21. Long, *Preaching from Memory to Hope*, 117.

the creation of a new world through Christ is the "through-line" of the theodrama and the glorious resolution and destination toward which the story has been moving (Isa. 65:17; Rom. 8:19–23; 2 Pet. 3:13; Rev. 21:1–2). The theodrama has a clear ending with the creation of the new heaven and earth and our lives in the New Jerusalem as citizens of God's kingdom. In order to convey the fullness of the gospel, pastors have a responsibility to point the church to God, who will judge the living and the dead on the last day. And yet God extends grace to us today through justification in Christ and the indwelling of the Spirit. To those who believe and commune with Christ, his return will be not a day of fear but a day of rejoicing and praise that today gives us hope, perspective, and vigilance to continue in the Spirit. The good news that we need to proclaim is the theological reality and implications of Christ's humiliation on the cross as well as his exaltation and eternal glory, which will be displayed for all to see when he returns.

Pastors can engage in prospection in preaching by considering the end of the Christian story. Of course, the church's story, confessions, and beliefs, and, more specifically, our own denominational nuances will flavor this contemplation. Questions may range from text-specific to broad reflections on eschatology: How should this text be understood in its immediate context but also against the backdrop of the greater theodrama and its conclusion? What is God doing in or behind this text toward the fulfillment of his plan? What does this text say about God's people living in this world as aliens and sojourners? How are we instructed to live in light of Christ's victory on the cross over sin, death, and evil and his promised second coming? What impact does eschatological hope have on our lives? How does it shape our understanding of missions? How does this text reorient our understanding of ourselves, our congregation, and our current circumstances and experiences?

Prospection is the practice of setting and resetting our eyes on the finish line by remembering the shape of the theodramatic plot. Knowing the story's end makes us live watchfully, single-mindedly, joyfully, and courageously, numbering our days, being rooted in Christ, prioritizing God's kingdom, and being all the more eager to meet with other believers to encourage one another as the final day draws near (Heb. 10:25). Our faith is built up in our acknowledgment of our own finitude and limitation, and as we lean in to expectantly live for God's kingdom, which will be fully realized with Christ's second coming. Prospection nurtures perspective, endurance, and hope as we anticipate and look forward to the theodrama's culmination. Until then, we live daily rehearsing our parts as "little Christs," and we find that we are "being transformed into the same image [of Christ] from one degree of glory to another" (2 Cor. 3:18).

We must practice the four perspectives together because, as vital as prospection is, sermons that rely only on it tend to foster fear, confusion, and disorder rather than faith, hope, and love. If our understanding of God's covenantal love does not precede our knowledge of the last days, we have no comfort in facing the Judge. Our sermons might frighten or alarm people into behaving well, but since those actions do not come from a transformed heart that has encountered the living Word, they are futile, meaningless, and temporary. We must preach the fullness of the gospel by making known the full scope of the theodrama, not only its parts. This does not mean that we have to recite the entire biblical story from the beginning to the end in our sermons every week, but a holistic theological thinking about Scripture should frame our sermon preparation and, beyond that, undergird our speech and enactment in preaching. Sidney Greidanus asserts: "A holistic interpretation of biblical texts demands further that the interpreter see the message of the text . . . in its broadest possible context, that is, Scripture's teaching regarding history as a whole. Frequently, this universal historical context is overlooked. There is no doubt, however, that Scripture teaches one universal kingdom history that encompasses all of created reality: past, present, and future."[22] Everything we do in the pulpit communicates theology. The question is, What kind of "God talk" are we currently modeling for our congregations, and where do we want to go from here?

The church does not despair or give up in the face of distractions, turmoil, adversity, and changing seasons because our eyes are fixed on the promise of the bridegroom who says he will return with his angels as the reigning King (Rev. 19:7–9; 21:1–4). When that day comes, the church, who is clothed in Christ's perfect righteousness and adorned with his glory,

---

22. Sidney Greidanus, *The Modern Preacher and the Ancient Text: Interpreting and Preaching Biblical Literature* (Grand Rapids: Eerdmans, 1988), 94–95.

will partake in the marriage feast that it did not merit. On that day, our earthly rehearsal will finally come to an end, and our only fitting response to this extravagant grace is endless praise and adoration, joining in the doxology of the renewed creation. That we can enjoy God forever is a gift of his unmerited kindness.

Index

DATE DUE

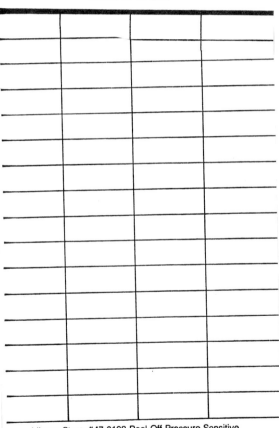